Heinemann
ASSEMBLY
Resources

Active Readings

for Assemblies

Peter Norton

Heinemann Educational Publishers
Halley Court, Jordan Hill, Oxford OX2 8EJ
a division of Reed Educational & Professional Publishing Ltd
Heinemann is a registered trademark of Reed Educational &
Professional Publishing Ltd

OXFORD MELBOURNE AUCKLAND
JOHANNESBURG BLANTYRE GABORONE
IBADAN PORTSMOUTH NH (USA) CHICAGO

ISBN 0 435 302310

04 03 02 01 00
10 9 8 7 6 5 4 3 2 1

Typeset and Illustrated by TechType, Abingdon, Oxon

Cover design by Brian Melville, Big Red Hat Design

Printed and bound in Great Britain by The Bath Press Ltd, Bath

Acknowledgements

The authors and publishers would like to thank the following for the
use of copyright material: Help the Aged for the log on p. 115;
Oxfam GB for the logo on p. 124: For more information about
Oxfam contact: Supporter Information Team, Oxfam GB, 274
Banbury Road, Oxford, OX2 7DZ www.oxfam.org.uk/coolplanet; The
Royal Society for the Protection of Birds for the logo on p. 133 and
© 1986 PANDA symbol WWF – World Wide Fund for Nature
(formerly World Wildlife Fund) for the information on p. 137.

The publishers have made every effort to trace the copyright
holders, but if they have inadvertently overlooked any, they will be
pleased to make the necessary arrangements at the first
opportunity.

Contents

Introduction

Assemblies provide an important opportunity for the development of the pupils' spiritual, moral, social and cultural awareness, as well as their 'Education for Citizenship'. To maximize the potential for pupils to progress in these areas it is important that the assemblies are presented in an interesting and lively way. This will make the pupils more likely to take note of the message behind the assembly. Assemblies can be made more visually stimulating by using OHP transparencies and involving the pupils in as many ways as possible: for example, by performing mini-plays, giving readings or by playing word games.

In these assemblies I have provided the essential factual information and some brief suggestions for interesting methods of delivery. When preparing signs for visual display, I suggest you use large sheets of paper and write the words on them in large, clear letters. Where questions are put to the pupils, an appropriate answer has been included *in italics*.

Many of these assemblies can be given a further spiritual element if, at the end, the pupils are asked to sit in silence for a moment and reflect (pray) on the message of the assembly.

The messages within each assembly can be further developed by making use of follow up PHSE – or in some cases RE – lessons. For this purpose I have included, where appropriate, some suggestions for activities you could use.

There are many pieces of music – both classical and contemporary – that can be played with each assembly, but the following pieces go particularly well with the suggested assemblies.

Assembly	Music
In the beginning	'Morning has broken' (Cat Stevens)
Exodus from Egypt	*Aida* by Giuseppi Verdi
Jesus goes into the desert	'Samba Pa Ti' (Santana)
Entry into Jerusalem	'Light of the world' (Jay Hamburger and Peggy Gordon)
Resurrection to ascension	'Heaven on their minds' by Andrew Lloyd-Webber and Tim Rice
The prodigal son	'No son of mine' (Genesis)
The rich fool	'Money, Money, Money' (Abba)
Harvest	'Harvest for the world' (Isley Brothers)
The lion and the mouse	'Circle of Life' (Elton John)

The miser	'Money' (Pink Floyd)
The north wind and the sun	'Sun arise' (Rolf Harris)
The mice and the weasels	'Dedicated follower of fashion' (Kinks)
The boy and the wolf	'Both sides of the story' (Phil Collins)
Roger Bannister	'Chariots of Fire' (Vangelis)
Mohandas (Mahatma) K Gandhi	'Song of India' by Rimsky-Korsakov
Martin Luther King Jr	'Ebony and Ivory' (Paul McCartney and Stevie Wonder)
Mary Jones	'Land of my fathers' by James James
Nelson Mandela	'Biko' (Peter Gabriel)
Ernest Shackleton	'Albatross' (Fleetwood Mac)
Abraham Lincoln and William Wilberforce	*Spartacus* by Aram Khachaturian
Terry Waite	'The Lebanon' (Human League)
Simon Weston	'Men of Harlech' by Thomas Oliphant
Dick Whittington (Lord Mayor of London)	'Streets of London' (Ralph McTell)
Emmeline Pankhurst	*Evita* by Andrew Lloyd-Webber and Tim Rice
Barnardo's Charity	'Driving the last spike' (Genesis)
The Royal National Institute for the Blind	'Blinded by the light' (Manfred Mann's Earth Band)
The Royal National Lifeboat Institution	'Titanic' by James Horner
The Royal Society for the Protection of Birds	'Snow Bird' (Anne Murray)
Save the Children	'Save the Children' (Marvin Gaye)
World Wide Fund for Nature	'Free Willy 1' (Michael Jackson)
Friends of the Earth	'Thinking of the Trees' (Enya)
Shelter	'Another Day in Paradise' (Phil Collins)

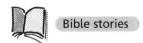

Bible stories

As well as playing their obvious role in the development of the pupils' *spiritual* awareness, many stories from the Bible can be used to increase the pupils' *moral* awareness (e.g. the prodigal son – forgiveness), as well as their *cultural* awareness (e.g. the temptation of Jesus – Lent). Using some of the stories about the miracles performed by Jesus, it is also possible to increase the pupils' sense of awe and wonder.

Assembly	Theme
In the beginning	The Christian story of God creating the Earth
Exodus from Egypt	Moses leads the Jewish people out of Egypt
The ten commandments	Rules and laws
Jesus goes into the desert	Temptation
Jesus sends out the twelve	The twelve disciples
A day of miracles	Miracles
Entry into Jerusalem	Jesus' entry into Jerusalem (Palm Sunday)
Resurrection to ascension	Events in Jesus' life after his resurrection
The prodigal son	Forgiveness
The rich fool	Money can't buy happiness
Parable of the talents	Making use of your talents
Judge no one	Do not judge someone merely by their appearance
A tree and its fruit	Choose your friends wisely
Harvest	Be thankful for plentiful food supplies

In the beginning

Theme

The Christian story of God creating the Earth

Materials

- Six large sheets of paper, each with one of the following words written on it:
  - Light
  - Land, sea and plants
  - Creatures of the air and sea
  - Sky
  - Sun, stars and moon
  - Humans

Assembly organization

Ask for six volunteers to come forward and hold up the six sheets of paper. Explain to the pupils that, using these words, you would like to talk to them about the Christian story of how God created the Earth.

As you go through the story, ask the pupils what God created next, then move that word into the correct order.

The following notes can be used to explain the story or, alternatively, at each stage the appropriate verses can be read from the Bible.

In the beginning

On the first day – Light

God created the universe and the Earth, then God said, 'Let there be light,' and it was light. God then divided the day into night and day.

[Genesis 1:1–5]

On the second day – Sky

God created the dome which formed the sky above the Earth.

[Genesis 1:6–8]

On the third day – Land, sea and plants

God made the seas separate from the land and on the land all kinds of plants started to grow.

[Genesis 1:9–13]

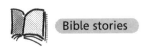

On the fourth day – Sun, stars and moon

God filled the night sky with stars and made the sun and moon.

[Genesis 1:14–19]

On the fifth day – Creatures of the air and sea

God filled the seas with fish and the air with birds.

[Genesis 1:20:23]

On the sixth day – Humans

God made animals of the land. He then made a man and called him Adam. From the man he made a woman to go with him and called her Eve.

[Genesis 1:26–31]

Ask what God did on the seventh day. *Rested.*

This is why Sunday is often called the day of rest.

Conclusion

Explain to the pupils that there are many beliefs about how the world began. This Biblical story explains how God created the Earth and everything on it, as well as everything in the universe, in six days.

You could also remind the pupils that there are many other ideas about how the Earth and the Universe were formed, and that we should respect each other's beliefs.

Follow-up activity

- Hold a brief class discussion about the ways in which people are polluting the Earth. Point out that the Earth is a very special planet, as it is the only one on which life is known to exist or believed to have been created.

- Ask the pupils to design a poster to encourage people not to pollute the Earth.

Exodus from Egypt

Theme

Moses leads the Jewish people out of Egypt

Materials

None necessary

Assembly organization

The events of this story could be made into a small mini-play with the pupils miming the actions.

Explain to the pupils that you are going to talk to them about a story from the Bible. At the end of the story you would like someone to tell you which story it is.

The following notes can be used to explain the story or, alternatively, you could read the appropriate sections from the Bible.

Exodus from Egypt

While he was looking after a flock of sheep in the desert, Moses saw a burning bush. He went nearer and he heard a voice telling him to go to Egypt to free the Jewish people.

[Exodus 3:1–21]

Moses set off for Egypt. On the way he met his brother Aaron.

Moses and Aaron went to see Pharaoh and asked him to release the Jewish people. Pharaoh refused. To show Pharaoh the power of their God, Aaron threw his stick on the ground and it turned into a snake. Moses and Aaron left Pharaoh.

[Exodus 7:1–13]

God told Moses to go back to Pharaoh and ask him again to release the Jewish people. If he refused, Moses was to ask his brother to pass his stick over the River Nile to turn it to blood. Once again Pharaoh refused. Having done as God told them, Moses and Aaron left Pharaoh.

[Exodus 7:14–24]

God told Moses to go back to Pharaoh. If he still would not release the Jewish people, Aaron was to wave his stick over the river, causing a plague of frogs to come up out of the water. Again Pharaoh refused. Having done as God told them, Moses and Aaron left Pharaoh.

[Exodus 8:1–15]

God told Moses to go back to Pharaoh once again. If Pharaoh would not let the Jewish people go, Aaron was to strike the ground with his stick, causing a plague of gnats to cover the ground. Pharaoh again refused. Once more Moses and Aaron did as God told them and then left Pharaoh.

[Exodus 8:16–19]

God sent Moses back again and again causing many more plagues, including flies [Exodus 8:20–24], the death of Egyptian animals [Exodus 9:1–7], boils [Exodus 9:8–12], hail [Exodus 9:13–35], locusts [Exodus 10:1–20] and darkness [Exodus 10:21–29]. Still Pharaoh refused to let the Jewish people go.

Finally, God told Moses to tell the Jewish people to mark their doors using lambs' blood. That night God sent his last plague, in which every firstborn of the Egyptians and their animals died, but because of the blood painted on the doors the Jewish people were not affected.

[Exodus 11:1–10, Exodus 12:21–29]

After this plague Pharaoh told Moses to take the Jewish people away.

[Exodus 12:30–33]

Ask what Bible story this is. *Moses and the exodus from Egypt.*

After letting the Jewish people go, Pharaoh had second thoughts. Ask the pupils what finally happened to let the Jewish people escape. *With God's help, Moses parted the Red Sea, letting the Jewish people escape and drowning the Egyptian Army.*

[Exodus 14:10–31]

Conclusion

Explain to the pupils that this story of how Moses and the Jewish people escaped from slavery under the Egyptian Pharaoh is celebrated in the Jewish feast of the Passover.

Follow-up activity

- Talk to the pupils about the times in recent history when other groups of people have been forced to leave their homes.

- Ask the pupils to imagine that they are going to be forced to leave home tomorrow. They can take with them only the things that they can carry. What items would they take with them? Why would they take those things?

The ten commandments

Theme

Rules and laws

Materials

- Ten sheets of paper, each with one of the ten commandments (given in the assembly) written on it

Assembly organization

Start by asking the pupils these questions.

- Who gave out the ten commandments? *God.*
- Who were the ten commandments given to? *Moses.*
- Where was Moses given the ten commandments? *Mount Sinai.*

Tell the pupils the story of how God gave Moses the ten commandments. If you wish, you could read the appropriate section from the Bible.

As each commandment is mentioned, you could read it from the Bible.

[Exodus 20:1–17]

After each of the commandments, you could give a little additional explanation about some of the terms the pupils might not know, such as idol, Sabbath, adultery.

The ten commandments

God came down to the top of Mount Sinai and called Moses to the top of the mountain. God told Moses to go and tell the rest of the people not to try to come up the mountain. Then God gave Moses the ten commandments.

[Exodus 19:20–25]

Ask the pupils what the ten commandments are, in the correct order. As each of the commandments is mentioned ask for a volunteer to hold up the correct sign.

1 Worship no god but me.
2 Do not make or worship idols.
3 Do not use my name for evil purposes.

4   Observe the Sabbath and keep it holy.
5   Respect your mother and father.
6   Do not commit murder.
7   Do not commit adultery.
8   Do not steal.
9   Do not accuse anyone falsely.
10   Do not desire another person's belongings.

You could also add to this list the extra commandment Jesus gave to his disciples: 'Love one another.'

[John 13: 34–35]

Explain that this could mean caring for all people, not just yourself. (You could also produce this as a poster to show in the assembly.)

Conclusion

Remind the pupils that Christians believe that these commandments are the laws given by God to Moses for the people to follow, but that also they are the basis of many countries' legal and moral beliefs.

Follow-up activity

- Start by reminding the class of the list of the ten commandments and the extra one Jesus gave to his disciples.

- Divide the class into small groups and ask them to divide the commandments into those that they think are religious, those that are moral and those that are legal. After a short while bring the class together and discuss the three different groupings they have produced.

Jesus goes into the desert

Theme

Temptation

Materials

None necessary

Assembly organization

Ask the pupils these questions.

• What special name is given to the day after pancake day? *Ash Wednesday.*

• What period of the Christian calendar begins on Ash Wednesday? *Lent.*

• What does Lent commemorate? *The time when Jesus went into the desert and was tempted by the Devil.*

Explain to the pupils more about the temptation of Jesus, either by using the following information or by reading the appropriate sections from the Bible.

If you wish, Jesus' replies to the Devil could be read out by a pupil.

The temptation of Jesus

After he had been baptized by John the Baptist, Jesus was led by the Holy Spirit into the desert. For forty days Jesus was in the desert, during which time he neither ate nor drank. Then the Devil appeared to Jesus. The Devil said to Jesus, 'If you are the son of God, turn these stones into bread.' Jesus replied,

'Human beings cannot live on bread alone, but need every word that God has said.'

[*Matthew 4:1–4*]

Then the Devil took Jesus to Jerusalem and up to the highest point on the temple, where he said to Jesus, 'If you are the son of God throw yourself off this tower and the angels will come down and hold you.'

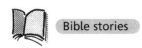

Jesus replied,

'Do not put the Lord your God to the test.'

[*Matthew 4: 5–7*]

Finally the Devil took Jesus to a very high mountain and said, 'All this I will give to you, if you will kneel down and worship me.' Jesus replied,

'Worship the Lord your God and serve only him.'

[*Matthew 4:8–11*]

Conclusion

Tell the pupils that following his forty days in the desert Jesus began his work, spreading the word of God and carrying out many miracles. This eventually led to his crucifixion and resurrection.

End the assembly by reminding the pupils that the period of the year called Lent is when Christians remember the time Jesus spent in the desert being tempted by the Devil.

Follow-up activity

- Divide the class into small groups. Ask them to think of occasions when they could be tempted by their friends to do something wrong. Following this, hold a short class discussion on the different forms of temptation.

- Ask the pupils to write a brief conversation between themselves and a friend who is trying to get them to do one of these things. In their work they should include things they might think – or say – that would help them resist the temptation to do as their friend is suggesting.

Jesus sends out the twelve

Theme

The twelve disciples

Materials

- Twelve large sheets of paper, each with one of the following names written on it:

  - Peter
  - James
  - Philip
  - Matthew
  - James
  - Judas

  - Andrew
  - John
  - Bartholomew
  - Thomas
  - Simon
  - Judas (Iscariot)

[Luke 6:12–16]

Assembly organization

Tell the pupils the following information, or read the relevant verses from the Bible.

Jesus sends out the twelve

Jesus called together the twelve disciples and gave them the power and authority to drive out all demons. They then set out and went from village to village preaching the gospel and healing people.

[Matthew 10: 1–15]

Ask the pupils to name the twelve disciples. As each one is named, ask for a volunteer to come forward and hold up the appropriate name and tell the pupils a few facts about that person.

Peter (St Peter)

Called Peter by Jesus, but was originally called Simon.

[Matthew 16:13–20]

After Jesus was taken prisoner Peter denied knowing him, as Jesus had predicted he would.

[Luke 22: 54–62]

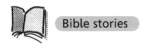

Andrew (St Andrew)

Peter's brother – they were both called to become disciples together when they were fishing by the Sea of Galilee.

[Matthew 4:18–20]

Patron Saint of Scotland.

John (St John)

He wrote the gospel of John. He was called to become a disciple, by the Sea of Galilee, after Peter and Andrew.

[Matthew 4:21–22]

When he was dying on the cross, Jesus entrusted the safety of his mother to John.

[John 19:26–27]

James the greater (St James)

He was the brother of John. With Peter and John, he witnessed the transfiguration of Jesus.

[Luke 9:28–36]

James was put to death by Herod Agrippa. He was the first disciple to die.

[Acts 12:1–2]

Thomas (St Thomas)

He is often called Doubting Thomas, because he refused to believe Jesus had risen from the dead until he saw the nail holes for himself.

[John 20:24–29]

Matthew (St Matthew)

Originally he was a tax collector but was called by Jesus.

[Matthew 9:9–13]

He wrote the gospel of Matthew.

Judas Iscariot

He betrayed Jesus.

[Luke 22:3–6]

Judas (Thaddaeus, St Jude)

Judas was also known as Jude (St Jude) or Thaddaeus, to avoid confusion with Judas Iscariot.

Legends suggest that he preached in Mesopotamia and Persia, where he was put to death.

Simon (St Simon)

He was called 'the Zealot' because he was a member of a group of people who were trying to overthrow the Roman occupiers of his country.

Some stories suggest that he preached in Persia with St Jude, where he was also put to death.

Philip (St Philip)

It is believed that he was an early follower of John the Baptist.

St Philip preached in Asia Minor where he was put to death.

James the lesser (St James)

He became the first Bishop of Jerusalem, where he was put to death.

Bartholomew (St Bartholomew)

He is believed to have travelled in India, Asia and Armenia where he was put to death.

Conclusion

Remind the pupils that, with the exception of Judas Iscariot, these disciples were the people who, after Jesus had risen and gone to heaven, went out and started to spread the teachings of Jesus.

Follow-up activity

- Hold a full-class discussion to generate a list of saints' names.

- Divide the class into small groups and ask them, using the names that have already been mentioned, to decide upon a definition of a saint.

- Bring the whole class together to agree a definition.

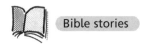

A day of miracles

Theme

Miracles

Materials

- Three large sheets of paper, each with one of the following sayings written on it:
  - Heals the sick
  - Feeds the five thousand
  - Walks on water

Assembly organization

Talk to the pupils about the idea that one of the ways Jesus showed himself to be special was by carrying out miracles.

Next talk to the pupils about the following miracles, which Jesus carried out all in the same day. Alternatively, you could read the verses from the Bible. As you introduce each of the miracles, ask for a volunteer to come forward and hold up the appropriate sign.

A day of miracles

Heals the sick

Having heard of the death of John the Baptist (Jesus' cousin and the person who had baptized Jesus), Jesus tried to go away to a lonely place. However, he found he was being followed by a large crowd. Taking pity on the people, he healed those who were sick.

[*Matthew 14:13–14*]

Feeds the five thousand

Later that same evening the disciples came to Jesus and suggested that, as it was getting late, the crowd should be sent away to find food. Jesus explained to the disciples that the crowd did not need to be sent away, but that they would feed them.

The disciples pointed out that they only had five loaves and two fishes, which would not be enough. Jesus asked that the loaves and fishes be brought to him, then he told the crowd to sit down on the grass. Jesus held the food up to heaven, blessed it, then gave it to the disciples to pass round, which they did. Everyone had enough to eat and at the end, when all the bits were picked up, there were twelve baskets of broken pieces left over.

In total they had fed five thousand men, not counting the women and children.

[Matthew 14:15–21]

Walks on water

As evening came on Jesus told the disciples to get into a boat while he dismissed the crowd. When the crowd had gone he went up onto a mountain to pray. By this time the disciples were a long way out on the lake.

The boat started to be buffeted by waves as a large storm had blown up. Jesus, walking on the water, went out to the disciples and told them to take courage and not to be afraid.

Seeing Jesus walking on the water, Peter tried to do the same but, becoming afraid, he started to sink. Jesus caught hold of him and asked why he had so little faith.

[Matthew 14:22–31]

You might like to end the assembly by asking the pupils to give some other examples of miracles carried out by Jesus.

Conclusion

Remind the pupils that these were just three of the many miracles carried out by Jesus during the time that he was on Earth.

Follow-up activity

- Divide the class into small groups. Ask them to remember the miracles performed by Jesus that were mentioned in the assembly, and any additional ones they can think of.

- Hold a whole class discussion to produce a list of the miracles.

- Divide the class back into the same small groups and give each group one of the miracles. Ask them to find out more about it.

- Ask each group to report what they have found about each of the miracles.

The following list of miracles and Bible references may be useful.

Miracle	Bible reference
Healing	
Leper	Luke 5:12–13
Centurion's servant	Luke 7:1–10
Peter's mother-in-law	Luke 4:38–39
Two Gadarenes	Luke 8:27–35
Paralysed man	Luke 5:18–25
Two blind men	Matthew 9:27–31
Dumb and possessed man	Matthew 9:32–33
Man with a withered hand	Luke 6:6–10
Boy with epilepsy	Luke 9:38–43
Bartimaeus the blind man	Luke 18:35–43
Deaf and dumb man	Mark 7:31–37
Blind man at Bethsaida	Mark 8:22–26
Woman bent double	Luke 13:11–13
Ten lepers	Luke17:11–19
Man born blind	John 9
Command over the forces of nature	
Calming storm	Luke 8:22–25
Walking on water	John 6:19–21
Four thousand people fed	Mark 8:1–9
Coin in fish's mouth	Matthew 17:24–27
Withered fig tree	Mark 11:12–14
Bringing back the dead	
Jairus' daughter	Luke 8:41–42
Widow's son	Luke 7:11–15
Lazarus	John 11:1–44

Entry into Jerusalem

Theme

Jesus' entry into Jerusalem (Palm Sunday)

Materials

- A palm cross
- A palm plant
- Two large sheets of paper, each with one of the following words written on it:
  - Jerusalem
  - Donkey

Assembly organization

Ask for a volunteer to come to the front and hold up a palm cross.

Ask the pupils which story from the Bible this object represents. *Jesus' entry into Jerusalem, Palm Sunday.*

Call three more volunteers to the front of the assembly. Ask them to hold up the two sheets of paper and the plant.

Ask for another volunteer to come out and put the objects into the correct order to tell the story. Then tell the appropriate part of the story for each of the objects, or you could read the sections from the Bible.

Entry into Jerusalem

Donkey

When they were near the towns of Bethphage and Bethany, Jesus sent two of his disciples ahead of him into the village. He said that in the town they would find a donkey and that they should untie it and bring it to him. If anyone asked them what they were doing they should reply that their master needed the animal. When they entered the village the disciples found the donkey just as Jesus had predicted. As they untied it, a group of bystanders asked what they were doing and they answered them just as Jesus had told them to do.

[Mark 11:1–6]

Palm plant

A large crowd had gathered in the city for the Festival of the Passover. When they heard that Jesus was coming they pulled down palm leaves and laid them on the floor, shouting, 'Praise God! God bless him who comes in the name of the Lord! God bless the King of Israel!'

[John 12:12–13]

Jerusalem

Just as it had been predicted in the scriptures, Jesus entered the city of Jerusalem riding on a donkey. The Pharisees were worried by this large crowd praising Jesus in this way.

[John 12:14–19]

Because of their fear of the influence Jesus was having, the Pharisees hatched a plot to arrest Jesus and have him crucified.

Conclusion

Talk to the pupils about these events being commemorated on the day we call Palm Sunday, which is held on the Sunday before Easter.

Follow-up activity

- Ask the pupils to write the story of Jesus' entry into Jerusalem, as seen by one of the people in the crowd.

- Explain to the pupils that they should include comments about what they see, about what is happening around them and about their feelings.

Resurrection to ascension

Theme
Events in Jesus' life after his resurrection

Materials
- Five large sheets of paper, each with one of the following sayings written on it:
  - On the road to Emmaus
  - Doubting Thomas
  - Ascension
  - Jesus appears to the disciples
  - Jesus' last miracle

Assembly organization
Explain to the pupils that many people know a great deal about the events surrounding Easter, but that fewer people know much about the events that took place in Jesus' life following his resurrection.

Talk to the pupils about the events following Jesus' resurrection. You could read the appropriate section from the Bible.

As you talk about each of the events call one volunteer to the front to hold up the appropriate sign. Alternatively, each of these stories could be made into a small mini-play where the pupils mime the actions.

Resurrection to ascension

On the road to Emmaus
After the crucifixion of Jesus, two of his followers were walking along the road to Emmaus. They were joined by a stranger whom they did not recognize. The stranger asked them what they were talking about and they explained to him the events of the last few days of Jesus' life. As it was late when they arrived at Emmaus, the two men invited the stranger to come and eat with them. At the meal table they recognized that the stranger was Jesus.

[*Luke 24:13–33*]

Jesus appears to the disciples
When the two followers (in the above story) returned to Jerusalem they explained to the disciples about their meeting with Jesus. While they were doing this, Jesus appeared to them. The disciples were afraid and thought they were seeing a ghost. To calm them, Jesus

showed them the nail holes in his hands and feet and even ate some boiled fish with them, which a ghost would not be able to do.

[*Luke 24:36–49*]

Doubting Thomas

When the others told Thomas what had happened he refused to believe it until he saw the nail holes himself and could put his fingers into them. (This is why he is often called Doubting Thomas.) Later on Jesus also appeared to Thomas and offered him his hands to put his fingers into the nail holes.

[*John 20:24–29*]

Jesus' last miracle

Peter had been a fisherman before Jesus called him. After Jesus had been crucified, Peter decided to go fishing. Some of the other disciples decided to go with him. They had been out fishing for some time and they had caught no fish. Each time they hauled in their net it was empty.

Once again Jesus appeared to them but they did not recognize him. He asked if they had caught any fish. 'No,' they replied. He told them to cast their net once more over the right side of their boat. This time their net was so full of fish they could hardly pull in the net.

When they came ashore they realized the stranger was Jesus. They all ate some of the fish Jesus had cooked.

[*John 21:1–14*]

Ascension

Jesus went with the disciples to Bethany where he blessed them. Then, raising his hands, Jesus was taken up into heaven. After this the disciples returned to Jerusalem.

[*Luke 24:50–53*]

Conclusion

Remind the pupils that these are some of the events that took place after the resurrection of Jesus and before he ascended into heaven, leaving the disciples to spread his teachings.

Follow-up activity

- Ask the pupils to write a conversation between one of the disciples and Thomas, where the disciple tells Thomas they have seen Jesus and that he is alive.

The prodigal son

Theme
Forgiveness

Materials
- Three large sheets of paper, each with one of the following words written on it:
  - Forgive
  - and
  - forget

Assembly organization
The events of this story could be made into a small mini-play where the pupils mime the actions.

Tell the pupils that you want them to listen to a story from the Bible. Afterwards, you want someone to tell you which story it is, and the message behind the story.

The parable of the prodigal son
There was once a rich man who had two sons. One day his younger son came and asked his father to give him his share of the family's wealth. The father divided up the family belongings and gave half to his younger son, who sold them all, took the money and left home. He travelled to a distant country where he squandered the money.

When a famine hit the country where he was living, the younger son had spent all his money and had nothing left to live on. He was starving. He went and found himself a job with a rich family, who gave him the task of looking after the pigs.

The younger son was so hungry he would have gladly eaten the food given to the pigs. He soon realized that the servants in his family's house were better off than he was. He decided to go home and ask his father to give him a job as a servant.

When he was still a long way from home, his father saw his son approaching and ran out to meet him. The son asked his father to let him be one of the family's servants, but instead the father sent his servants to get new clothes and to prepare a feast.

Hearing of the preparations for the celebration, the elder son came to his father to complain. The father pointed out that the son he thought was dead had returned home and that this was cause for celebration.

[Luke 15:11–32]

Ask which story this is from the Bible. *The parable of the prodigal son.*

Ask what is the meaning of the story. *Forgiveness.*

Bring three volunteers out to the front to hold up the words and ask someone to come forward and make a saying related to the message of this parable. *Forgive and forget.*

Conclusion

Explain to the pupils the meaning of the above saying and talk to them about the occasions when they should forgive people:

- after arguments with friends
- after arguments with their parents.

Follow-up activity

- Ask the pupils to write a conversation between two people, in which one person is trying to persuade the other to forgive someone else for what they have done. (Include in it what they are to forgive.)

  It might be a father or mother talking about forgiving a brother or sister, or a friend talking about forgiving another friend for what they have done.

- Some pupils could be asked to work with a friend and produce their conversation as a play, to perform in front of the rest of the class.

The rich fool

Theme

Money can't buy happiness

Materials

- Six large sheets of paper, each with one of the following written on it:
  - Money
  - Good looks
  - Health
  - Happiness
  - Friends
  - Intelligence

Assembly organization

Ask six volunteers to come out to the front and hold up the six signs. Ask for another volunteer to come and put them in order of importance.

Talk to the pupils about the order of importance the volunteer has chosen. Stress the value that should be placed on health and happiness and the lesser importance of money.

Emphasize this point by telling the pupils the following parable from the Bible. Alternatively, you could read the parable straight from the Bible. Explain to the pupils that you want them to listen to a parable from the Bible and afterwards you would like someone to explain what it means.

The parable of the rich fool

A man in the crowd asked Jesus to tell his brother to divide their family property between the two of them. In reply, Jesus told this parable.

There was a man whose fields produced large crops, but he was unsure what to do with all his wealth. He was concerned that he did not have enough space to store all his crops. This is what he decided to do.

He would pull down his existing store-house and build himself a new and bigger one, then he would collect all his crops and belongings and keep them in this new store-house.

Once all this was done he would say to himself, 'You now have enough wealth stored away for many years, so you can sit back and enjoy life.'

Bible stories

Then God said to the man, 'You fool! This very night you must surrender your life; you have made your money – who will get it now?'

Then Jesus said, 'This is how it is with a man who builds up wealth but who does not lead a good life in the eyes of God.'

[Luke 12:13–21]

Ask the pupils what they think Jesus meant by this parable. *It is more important to lead a good life than it is to build up a large fortune.*

Conclusion

Talk to the pupils about the fact that money cannot buy happiness. Explain that there are things in life which are more likely to bring you happiness and therefore are more important than just money.

Follow-up activity

- Hold a brief class discussion about the prices of various items you might want to buy as a lottery winner.

- Organize a lottery draw, in which each pupil draws out a piece of paper with an imaginary lottery win on it.

- Each pupil should write their own 'spending and saving' plan for the money they have won. They should show what they would buy and how much it would cost. They should think about savings and any money they would spend on friends and family or donate to charity.

Parable of the talents

Theme

Making use of your talents

Materials

• A large seed

Assembly organization

Talk to the pupils about several famous people, both past and present. Ask the pupils to identify what each person was famous for, and then to identify what talents they must have had to become famous. An example might be:

Michael Owen   Footballer   Fitness, good control of a football

Vanessa Mae   Violinist   Reads music, plays a violin

Tell the pupils the parable from the Bible. Alternatively, you could read the appropriate section from the Bible to the pupils.

The parable of the talents

A man was planning to go away on holiday. Before he did he called together three of his servants and gave each of them some of his money to look after.

He gave each servant a different amount of money. He gave the first servant 5000 coins, to the second he gave 2000 coins and to the third he gave 1000 coins. Then he went away.

The servant with 5000 coins invested it wisely and earned another 5000 coins, as did the second servant who earned another 2000 coins. The servant who had been given 1000 coins went and dug a large hole in which to bury the coins.

After some time, when the master returned, he sent for each servant. The first servant came to see the master with the original 5000 coins and the extra 5000 he had earned. The master was pleased with him.

In the same way, the second servant came forward with the original 2000 coins he had been given and the extra 2000 he had earned. Once again, the master was pleased.

Finally the master sent for the third servant who came forward and gave the master his 1000 coins but nothing extra. The master was annoyed and ordered that the lazy servant should be taken and thrown out of his house.

[*Matthew 25:14–30*]

Explain to the pupils that the meaning behind this parable is that we should always make the best of our talents. You could emphasize this point by holding up the seed and asking the pupils what it needs to germinate and grow. *Warmth, water, soil and light.* In just the same way their talents will not develop and grow without hard work, interest, enthusiasm, and so on.

Conclusion

Talk to the pupils about the importance of them all making the best of their talents and always trying their hardest at everything they do.

You could relate this back to the famous people you mentioned at the start of the assembly, making the point that they would not have become famous without hours of practice at the skills they each needed.

Follow-up activity

- Ask the pupils to design an illustrated poster using the heading 'Make the best use of your talents'.

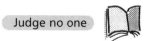

Judge no one

Theme

Do not judge someone merely by their appearance

Materials

- Two pairs of jeans which belong to the same person:
  - one pair dirty and torn
  - one pair clean and nearly new

Assembly organization

Ask for two volunteers to come forward and hold up the two pairs of jeans. Indicate each pair in turn and ask the pupils to make judgements about the person who owns them, based on their appearance only. This could be explained as being a police investigation, where they are trying to put together a picture of a suspect based on pieces of evidence. Some answers you may receive are:

Old jeans: *The person might be poor, untidy, dirty, unemployed…*

New jeans: *The person might be wealthy, tidy, clean, a businessman…*

If this exercise has been carried out as a police investigation you could end this part of the assembly by asking the pupils who they think committed the crime. *The owner of the dirty jeans.*

Conclude this part of the assembly by telling the pupils that the jeans actually belong to the same person. Ask what they have been guilty of, by making these judgements based only on the appearance of the jeans. *Prejudice.*

Next talk to the pupils about the following extract from the Bible, or read the appropriate section to them.

Warning against prejudice

A rich person wearing jewels and fine clothes comes to a meeting and a poor person in ragged clothes also comes to the same meeting.

You show respect to the rich person and offer them the best seat, but pay little attention to the poor person and tell them to stand at the back of the room.

Then you are guilty of making judgements for the wrong reasons.

You will be doing the right thing if you do what it says in the Bible, 'Love your neighbour as you love yourself.' If you judge people based only on their appearance then you are wrong.

[*James 2:1–9*]

You could also relate this idea to the parable of the Good Samaritan, told by Jesus.

[*Luke 10:25–37*]

Conclusion

Remind the pupils that they should never judge people purely by their appearance. They should wait to find out what the person is like before forming any opinions.

Follow-up activity

- Ask the pupils, in small groups, to decide whether the statements on the Prejudice questionnaire are true or false.

- Follow this by a whole-class discussion on the correct answers to the questionnaire.

Prejudice questionnaire

> **Look at each of these statements and decide if they are true or false.**
>
> 1   Many black people are British.
>
> 2   All gypsies are dishonest.
>
> 3   Women are not strong enough to drive big lorries.
>
> 4   Women are better cooks than men.
>
> 5   Not all football supporters are hooligans.
>
> 6   All politicians tell lies.
>
> 7   People with long hair and beards are troublemakers.
>
> 8   Overweight people do not always eat too much.
>
> 9   People who own Rolls Royce cars have well-paid jobs.
>
> 10   Only Reebok trainers are good quality.

A tree and its fruit

Theme

Choose your friends wisely

Materials

- Ten large sheets of paper, each with one of the following written on it:

  - Oak tree
  - Horse chestnut tree
  - Apple tree
  - Scots pine tree
  - Cherry tree

  - Acorns
  - Conkers
  - Apples
  - Fir cones
  - Cherries

Assembly organization

Ask for ten volunteers to come out to the front to hold up the tree signs and the seed signs. Ask another volunteer to come and match the trees to their seeds.

Next ask the pupils to listen to the following story from the Bible and to try to work out the message behind it. Alternatively, you could read the appropriate section from the Bible.

A tree and its fruit

A good tree does not bear bad fruit, neither does a bad tree bear good fruit. Each type of tree can be recognized by its fruit. You cannot collect figs from a thorn bush. The same is true of people. Good people bring only goodness out of the goodness in their hearts, while bad people bring only unkind things out of the unkindness in their hearts.

[*Luke 6: 43–45*]

Ask what this story means. *Good and kind people will behave in a good and kind way, while bad people will behave in an unkind and unpleasant way.*

Conclusion

Talk to the pupils about the importance of choosing good friends who will help you behave in sensible ways and of the importance of avoiding people who behave in unacceptable ways, because they will probably only get you into trouble.

You could relate this to these proverbs which could be read out by pupils:

- 'Keep company with the wise and you will become wise. If you make friends with stupid people, you will be ruined.'

[*Proverbs 13:20*]

- 'Stay away from foolish people; they have nothing to teach you.'

[*Proverbs 14:7*]

Follow-up activity

- Hold a class discussion about the qualities the pupils would expect from a good friend and the qualities they would associate with people who were not good friends, i.e. 'bad friends'.

- Using the headings 'Good friends' and 'Bad friends', the pupils could write a list of qualities they would expect to find in each type of friend.

Harvest

Theme

Be thankful for plentiful food supplies

Materials

- A collection of different fruits and vegetables. Also include Brazil nuts, bananas, avocado, coal and wood

Assembly organization

Start by talking about the different foods that you have at the front, explain where they come from, where they grow, etc.

Ask the pupils which festival celebrates the growth of all these foods? *Harvest Festival.*

Explain to the pupils that Harvest Festival held at this time of year has its origins in the statements (below) made by Moses to the Israelites. The statements could be read out by a pupil.

Harvest offerings

'Each of you must place in a basket the first part of each crop that you harvest and you must take it with you to one of the houses of worship.'

'Be grateful for the good things that the Lord your God has given you and your family.'

[*Deuteronomy 26:2,11*]

Ask the pupils why they think you have included coal and wood in the collection. *They are also things that are harvested from the Earth.*

Explain that in some churches coal is included in the collection of produce, as it is also seen as a gift from God for which we should give thanks.

You could point out that the harvesting of some types of wood, that come from the tropical rainforests, such as mahogany and teak (which are used in the making of furniture) are putting the whole survival of the rainforest environment in danger. To extract these valuable trees the whole forest is cut down. Every year an area the

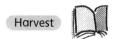

size of England, Scotland and Wales is cleared.

Next ask the pupils what is the difference between the Brazil nut, banana and the avocado and the other fruits and vegetables you have collected. *These originally grew in rainforests.*

Explain that, in fact, the Brazil nut still has to be collected from trees in the rainforest. There are believed to be many other fruits and vegetables which grow in rainforests, which could be grown and eaten. There are also many plants which contain helpful medicines – for example the Madagascan periwinkle contains a chemical which can help people suffering from leukaemia – but which we are in danger of losing because of the destruction of the forests.

Conclusion

Remind the pupils that we should be thankful for our plentiful food supplies and that we should always be aware of those peoples around the world who are less fortunate than ourselves. Many have to survive on poor food supplies and often face starvation every day.

You could also point out that in our harvests we should be aware of the need to live a sustainable lifestyle – one in which we do not take from the Earth more of its resources than we need – and we do not, in taking our harvest, destroy the environment from which it came.

Follow-up activity

- Ask the pupils to design a poster to show the world's produce that they are most grateful for.

Aesop's fables

Aesop's fables have been used for hundreds of years to tell moral messages. This makes them ideal for encouraging the pupils' moral development.

At some point in using these assemblies you might tell the pupils a little about Aesop. He was a Greek slave, who lived in the sixth century BCE (approximately 2600 years ago). He was eventually made a free man and then started travelling around Greece telling his stories, until he was invited to the court of King Croesus of Lydia.

Assembly	Theme
The donkey and its shadow	Arguments are pointless
Mercury and the woodsman	Honesty is the best policy
The beekeeper and the bees	Things are not always what they seem
The eagle and the beetle	Determination overcomes many problems
The fisherman and the sprat	Be satisfied with the things you have
The lion and the mouse	We all have different abilities which we should make use of fully
The miser	The joy of money is not in just owning it but in what you can do with it
The town mouse and the country mouse	People have different likes, dislikes and beliefs
The piping fisherman	Nothing is gained without hard work
The lamp	Pride comes before a fall
A man and his five sons	More can be achieved by working together than by working alone

Assembly	Theme
The stag and the pool	What is of most worth is not always of most value
The north wind and the sun	More can be gained by persuasion than by force
The thief and the dog	Beware of people who offer you a bribe
The mice and the weasels	Vanity can lead to your downfall
The boy and the wolf	The truth is not always obvious

The donkey and its shadow

Theme
Arguments are pointless

Materials
None necessary

Assembly organization
Ask the pupils to listen to the following story of the donkey and its shadow and explain that at the end you want someone to tell you the moral of the story.

The donkey and its shadow
A traveller hired a donkey to help him on his journey, having agreed the price with its owner. The owner said, 'There is only one problem, my donkey will not go far unless I hit him with a stick.'

So the two men agreed that it would be best if the traveller rode on the donkey, while the owner walked alongside and occasionally hit the donkey gently with his stick to keep it walking.

It was a very hot day and both men soon became tired. By midday they were both in need of a rest and they agreed to stop. The traveller got down off the donkey and said, 'I will sit here in the donkey's shadow.'

The owner said, 'No, you will not. I own the donkey so I own its shadow. I will sit here in the shade.'

The traveller explained, 'I have hired the donkey so today I own its shadow.'

The two men soon started to argue and even started to fight over who owned the right to sit in the donkey's shadow. While all this was happening they did not notice the donkey wander off.

Soon the donkey had wandered far away, taking his shadow with him, but still the two men continued to argue over who had the right to sit in the donkey's shadow.

Ask the pupils what the moral of this story might be. *Arguments are pointless.*

Ask the pupils how they think the men could have solved their problem without arguing. *By sharing the time in the shadow, for example, ten minutes each.*

Conclusion

Talk to the pupils about situations in their lives where arguments could occur. Suggest to them possible ways of avoiding arguments.

Follow-up activity

- Ask the pupils to rewrite the story of the donkey and its shadow but this time the two men solve the problem without arguing.

Mercury and the woodsman

Theme

Honesty is the best policy

Materials

- Five large sheets of paper, each with one of the following words written on it:
  - Honesty • is • the • best • policy

Assembly organization

This would be an ideal assembly to make into a mini-play acted out by pupils.

Ask for five volunteers to come out to the front and hold up the words of the saying in the wrong order. Next bring another volunteer and ask them to try to rearrange the words into a saying. To illustrate the meaning behind this saying, tell the pupils this fable.

Mercury and the woodsman

There once was a woodcutter who worked hard each day cutting wood in the forest. He always used his favourite axe which he kept clean and sharp.

One day he went into the woods to start his day's work, cutting down a tree by a deep, fast-flowing river. Unfortunately the woodcutter dropped his axe into the river and was unable to get it back.

'Help me!' he shouted. 'The water is too deep and fast-flowing for me to get my axe and without it I will not be able to work.'

Hearing the woodcutter's cries, the god Mercury flew down, dived into the river and brought up a golden axe.

'That is not my axe,' said the woodcutter.

Once again Mercury dived down into the water and came up, this time with a silver axe.

'That is not my axe,' said the woodcutter.

Once more Mercury dived down into the water and this time came up with an old axe.

'That is mine,' said the woodcutter.

Mercury was so impressed by the man's honesty that he gave him back his axe and the gold and silver axes as well.

This story was heard by another woodcutter. He went to the same river and dropped in his axe and started to cry for help. Once again Mercury heard the man's cries and came down to help him. He dived into the river and came up with a golden axe which the man immediately said was his axe.

Annoyed by the woodcutter's obvious lie, Mercury punished him by making the golden axe disappear and leaving the man's own axe at the bottom of the river.

Conclusion

Talk to the pupils about the moral of this story. Discuss examples of honesty in everyday life.

If you wish you could relate this moral to the proverb from the Bible:

'Honest people will lead a full and happy life.'

[Proverbs 28:20]

Follow-up activity

• Ask the pupils to write two short stories.

A child finds £50 in the street.

Write one story in which the child is honest in what he does with the money and one story in which he is dishonest.

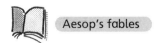

The beekeeper and the bees

Theme

Things are not always what they seem

Materials

None necessary

Assembly organization

Ask the pupils to listen to the fable. Tell them that afterwards you want someone to tell you the moral behind the story.

The beekeeper and the bees

A man once kept bees for their honey. He always took care of his bees and the hive. He never took all of the honey and always left some for the bees.

One day, after he had gone to dinner and while the bees were out searching for pollen to make their honey, a thief came along and broke into the hives, stealing all the honey and leaving everything in a terrible mess.

When he returned to find his hives in such a mess the beekeeper was very upset and cried, 'My poor bees, what will they do with all their honey gone? I must put things straight for them before they get back.'

Then he started to collect all the broken parts of the hives and tried to put them back together.

While he was doing this the bees returned from their morning's work and saw the mess. They also saw the beekeeper who seemed to be the person who had caused all the damage and started to attack him, stinging him all over.

The beekeeper cried out in pain, 'Why do you attack me when I am trying to repair the damage done by someone else, who has gone away without a single sting?'

Ask the pupils what they think might be the moral of this fable.
Things are not always what they seem.

You could relate the moral of this fable to the parable of the Good Samaritan, in the Bible.

[*Luke 10:25–37*]

Conclusion

Talk to the pupils about the fact that people are not always what they seem and that they should not be judged just by their looks, beliefs or skin colour.

Follow-up activity

- Ask the pupils to produce an illustrated poster using the heading 'Never judge a book by its cover.'
- A more challenging activity would be to write a modern-day version of the Good Samaritan story.

The eagle and the beetle

Theme

Determination overcomes many problems

Materials

- A large sheet of paper with the following saying written on it:

  'If at first you don't succeed, try, try, try again.'

Assembly organization

Ask for a volunteer to come forward and hold up the sign. Ask the rest of the pupils if they can tell you what this saying means. *If things don't go right at first keep trying, don't just give up.*

Tell the pupils that you want them to listen to a fable which shows this point.

The eagle and the beetle

An eagle was out hunting one day when it saw a hare in a field. The eagle started to swoop down on the hare, with its claws extended ready to pounce. The hare saw the eagle and started to run, screaming for help, 'Help me! Help me someone!'

The only animal in the field at that time was a beetle. Hearing the hare's cries, the beetle felt sorry for it and offered to help. As the eagle swooped down, the beetle shouted out, 'Eagle! Do not touch that hare, he is under my protection.'

The eagle took no notice of the beetle, but caught the hare in its claws and carried it off to eat. The beetle was so annoyed by the eagle's actions that he decided to avenge the hare's death. So he climbed up into the eagle's nest and hid himself away.

Every time the eagle laid an egg, the beetle waited until the eagle flew away then he pushed the egg out of the nest, smashing it on the ground. This happened time and time again.

The beetle destroyed so many of the eagle's eggs that the eagle decided to do something about it, so he flew up to see the god Jupiter.

Jupiter said to the eagle, 'Lay your eggs in my lap, they will be safe there. The beetle will not dare to damage them while I am looking after them.'

When Jupiter said this, he did not allow for the determination of the beetle, who always finished what he started.

The beetle waited until the eagle had laid a full clutch of eggs. Then he rolled up a ball of earth and, unseen, placed it in Jupiter's lap. When he saw the soil Jupiter stood up, without a thought, and wiped the soil and the eggs out of his lap, smashing the eggs on the floor.

Once again the beetle had his way.

Conclusion

Talk to the pupils about occasions in life when they may need to show the same amount of determination that the beetle showed.

Remind the pupils always to remember the words of the saying you started with:

'If at first you don't succeed, try, try, try again.'

Follow-up activity

- Ask the pupils which personal quality the beetle showed. *Determination.*

- Ask the pupils to produce a poster (an example is shown below) using the word 'determination' and other words and phrases which mean the same as determination.

Words and phrases for this exercise can be found using a dictionary or thesaurus.

```
            D
 N  E  V  E  R      G  I  V  E     U  P
            T
            E
            R
            M
      F     I  R  M  N  E  S  S
            N
            A
            T
            I
            O
            N
```

The fisherman and the sprat

Theme
Be satisfied with the things you have

Materials
None necessary

Assembly organization
Tell the pupils the following two fables, during which you want them to see if they can decide what the moral is behind them.

The fisherman and the sprat
The weather had been awful all day, raining and blowing a gale, and a poor fisherman was having a bad day. He had set out at dawn and sailed far out to sea, casting his net over and over again. Each time he had hauled in the net it was empty. He started to wonder if there were any fish left in the sea.

He decided to try once more, so again he cast his net into the sea. This time when he hauled his net in there was something wriggling at the bottom. Excitedly he rushed to the end of the net to find what he had caught.

To his disgust the fisherman found only a tiny little fish.

'Please let me go,' begged the fish. 'I am too small for you to eat and if you let me go now you can catch me again in a year's time when I will be much bigger.'

'No way!' said the fisherman. 'If I let you go now I may never catch you again.'

(Ask the pupils to think about the moral in this story while they listen to the next one.)

The dog and his reflection

A dog had found a large, juicy piece of meat which he had taken and was carrying off somewhere safe to eat. As he went he had to cross a stream. Looking down he saw another dog with what he thought was a bigger juicier piece of meat.

So he opened his mouth to take the other dog's piece of meat.

Ask the pupils what it was that the dog saw in the water. *His reflection.*

Ask what happened when he tried to get the other piece of meat. *He dropped his piece of meat into the water.*

Ask the pupils what moral the two fables have in common. *Be satisfied with what you have.*

Ask if anyone can tell you a saying that has this same meaning. *A bird in the hand is worth two in the bush.*

Conclusion

Talk to the pupils about the importance of not envying other people's things and of being satisfied with what you have got.

If you wish you could relate this point to the tenth commandment, which says, 'Do not desire other people's possessions.'

[*Exodus 20:17*]

Follow-up activity

- Ask the pupils to produce an illustrated poster using one of the three sayings used in the assembly:
- Do not desire other people's possessions
- A bird in the hand is worth two in the bush
- Be satisfied with what you have.

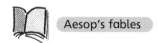

The lion and the mouse

Theme

We all have different abilities which we should make use of fully

Materials

- OHP and screen
- OHT 1 'The lion and the mouse'

Assembly organization

Display the OHT on the screen. Ask the pupils to identify the two animals. Ask the pupils what qualities these two animals have. *The lion – big, strong; the mouse – small, agile.*

Tell the pupils that you are going to read a story to them, and afterwards you want them to tell you the meaning.

The lion and the mouse

A lion was once sleeping peacefully in the jungle, when a mouse came creeping quietly past. Unfortunately the mouse disturbed the lion's sleep, who with one swipe pinned the mouse to the ground.

The lion was just about to take a second swipe at the mouse to kill it when the mouse pleaded for its life, saying, 'Please do not kill me. I am too small to make a meal and if you let me live I may be able to help you one day.'

The lion laughed at the thought of the tiny mouse being able to help him, but nevertheless decided to let the mouse go.

Later that day the lion was strolling along a jungle path when a net from a hunter's trap dropped on him. Unable to move, he could do nothing until the hunter returned.

After a short while the lion heard a rustling noise near by which he assumed was the hunter returning to collect him. To the lion's surprise it turned out to be the mouse who, recognizing the lion, came over and offered to help.

The lion started to laugh and said, 'The ropes that hold me down are too strong for me to break. So how can you help, little mouse?'

Without answering the mouse set to work gnawing through the ropes which held the lion down. After half an hour the mouse had made a hole big enough for the lion to escape. When he was free the lion thanked the mouse and then the two animals went their separate ways never to meet again.

Ask the pupils the moral of this fable. *We all have different talents.*

To emphasize this moral, you could talk to the pupils about famous people, past and present, and the different skills they have. This could be played as a game, using large sheets of paper with the names of the people and their different skills written on them. The pupils then match the skills to each person's name.

Conclusion

Talk to the pupils about different subjects within school, and the different skills they need within each of them. Make the point that different people do better in different subjects. Whatever we are good at, we should always develop our abilities to their full potential.

Follow-up activity

- Ask the pupils to work in pairs first to identify their own strengths and then to identify their partner's strengths.

- Next ask each pair to swap their opinions of each other's strengths.

- Then ask each pair to identify the strengths needed for each subject area.

- Each individual can use this information to predict which are their best subjects.

  This activity could be related to achievements mentioned in school reports.

OHT 1 'The lion and the mouse'

The miser

Theme

The joy of money is not in just owning it but in what you can do with it

Materials

- A large sheet of paper with the word 'Miser' written on it

Assembly organization

Ask for a volunteer to come to the front and hold up the sign with the word 'Miser' written on it. Ask the pupils what this word means. *A person who is mean with their money and keeps it all.*

Ask the pupils the name of the miser in Charles Dickens' novel 'A Christmas Carol'. *Ebenezer Scrooge.*

Continue asking the pupils questions about Ebenezer Scrooge.

At the start of the story what did Scrooge do with his money. *Saved it.*

Was he a happy person? *No.*

After the visit by the three ghosts, what did Scrooge start to do with his money? *Spend it.*

Was he a happy person then? *Yes.*

Ask the pupils to listen to the following fable and explain that at the end you want someone to tell you the moral.

The miser

A rich man once sold all his belongings. With his money he bought a large piece of gold. He took the gold and buried it under a huge rock. Each day the man went back to where his gold was buried and dug it up, looked at it, then buried it under the rock again and went away.

One day when the miser went to look at his gold another person saw him. This person waited until the miser had gone, then went and dug up the gold and stole it.

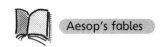

The next day when the miser came to look at his gold he found it had been stolen. In a panic he looked everywhere for his gold but he could not find it. Eventually he collapsed in a heap and started to cry.

When the miser told a friend why he was so upset the friend passed him a large stone and said, 'Why don't you bury this stone and dig it up each day? As you had no intention of spending the gold the stone will be of as much use to you.'

Ask the pupils what they think the moral of this fable might be. *The joy of money is not in just owning it but in what you can do with it.*

You could relate this to the parable of the rich fool, told by Jesus in the Bible.

[Luke 12:13–21]

Conclusion

Talk to the pupils about ways in which they can use their money to bring happiness to themselves and others, such as giving to charity or buying presents for parents.

Follow-up activity

• Ask the pupils to design a poster to encourage people to give money to their favourite charity.

The poster could include the sentence, 'Don't be a miser...'

The town mouse and the country mouse

Theme
People have different likes, dislikes and beliefs

Materials
- Different pieces of fruit
- Recordings of different pieces of music
- Tape recorder or CD player

Assembly organization
Tell the pupils the following fable and ask for someone at the end to tell you what is the moral.

The town mouse and the country mouse
A town mouse once went to visit his friend in the country. He was most disappointed when they went to get some food and his friend offered him some seeds, roots and berries. His disappointment grew to disgust when they went back to the country mouse's house to find it was a cold, wet hole at the bottom of a tree.

The town mouse said to the country mouse, 'What an unpleasant life you have. You have no proper food to eat and you live in this draughty old tree. You must come and stay with me and I will show you how well we live in the town.'

The country mouse was hurt by his friend's comments but agreed to go and visit his home in the town.

When they arrived in the town the country mouse agreed that life in the town really was wonderful: he had never seen so much food as was available in the kitchen. However the country mouse had just started to enjoy eating a nice juicy apple when his friend said, 'Come on! We must run! Someone is coming!'

The two mice hurried out of the kitchen and hid in a hole in the wall.

The town mouse found himself squashed up against the wall, unable to breathe.

After some time the town mouse decided it would be safe to go out, so the two mice crept out of the hole. Having stretched their legs and uncrumpled their whiskers, the country mouse went to pick up the apple he had been enjoying before they had been disturbed.

Before he could take another bite out of the apple, his friend said, 'Quick! Someone is coming again! We must hide!' Once again the two mice scurried into the hole in the wall.

'That's it!' said the country mouse. 'What's the point of all that lovely food if you can't enjoy eating it? I'm going back to the country. The food might not be as good but at least you can enjoy what you do get.'

Ask the pupils what the moral is behind this fable. *People have different likes and dislikes.*

Emphasize the moral by talking to the pupils about different people's tastes in fruit and music. You could make the point by offering pupils different pieces of fruit, or by playing different pieces of music.

Conclusion

Talk to the pupils about the fact that not only do people have different likes and dislikes, but that they also have different beliefs. We must accept that people can believe in different things, just as different people like different types of fruit or music.

Follow-up activity

- Ask the pupils to carry out a class survey of each other's likes and dislikes (for example in music, food, books).

- The results could be displayed as tables and charts to emphasize the saying 'Everybody is different.'

The piping fisherman

Theme
Nothing is gained without hard work

Materials
None necessary

Assembly organization
Before the assembly, ask a volunteer to practise a piece of music to play in the assembly.

This would be an ideal assembly to make into a mini-play in which a pupil acts out the fisherman's role.

Ask the pupils to listen to the fable, and see if they can work out the moral behind the story.

The piping fisherman
There was once a fisherman who also played the pipes. He desperately wanted to become a musician.

He much preferred to play his pipes rather than go out and work hard trying to catch fish. However, the only way he could make money was by throwing his nets into the sea and hauling them in, full of fish.

One day the fisherman took his pipes down to the sea with him. He said to himself, 'People say my music is so fine, perhaps if I cast my nets into the sea and then play, the fish will swim into my nets and I can catch them without having to work hard at all.'

So the fisherman cast his nets into the sea and then started to play his pipes.

(Ask your volunteer to play a tune.)

After a while the fisherman hauled in his nets, only to find them completely empty. In the end, disappointed and muttering to himself, the fisherman put his pipes away and went back to fishing.

He cast his nets into the water and when he hauled them in they were full of fish.

The fisherman wondered to himself why it was that when he played his pipes he didn't catch a single fish, but that when he was not playing his pipes he cast his nets and hauled them in full of fish.

Ask the pupils what the moral of this story could be. *Nothing is gained without hard work.*

You could relate this to the proverb in the Bible:

'Being lazy will make you poor, but hard work will make you rich.'

[*Proverbs 10:4*]

Conclusion

Talk to the pupils about the importance of working hard in all their lessons, so that whatever they achieve it will be their best. This is all anyone will ever expect of them.

Follow-up activity

- Start by talking to the pupils about the importance of working hard in all their lessons if they are going to fulfil their true potential.

- Next ask the pupils to complete the questionnaire.

- Finally, this activity could be rounded off by setting some target for improved effort in lessons or homework.

Questionnaire

How hard do you work? Start by writing down the subjects you are doing. For each subject, think how hard you work in lessons and how much effort you put into your homework. Put ticks in the correct columns. Be honest!

Subject	In lessons			Homework		
	Always work hard	Usually work hard	Never work hard	Always work hard	Usually work hard	Never work hard

The lamp

Theme

Pride comes before a fall

Materials

- A table lamp
- A table

Assembly organization

Explain to the pupils that you are going to tell them two fables. Afterwards you would like someone to tell you the connection between them both.

Before you start, switch on the table lamp and explain that the lamp in the original story would have been a lamp that burnt oil.

The lamp

A lamp was proudly boasting to its owner about itself, how bright and shiny it was and how brightly it shone. 'Look at me,' said the lamp. 'I really am the smartest thing in the room and I shine so brightly, brighter even than the stars and the moon.'

Just at that point a gust of wind blew in through an open window and blew out the lamp.

(Switch off the lamp.)

The room was in complete darkness.

The lamp's owner said to the lamp, 'How foolish you were, to compare yourself to the brightness of the stars and the moon. A little gust of wind can blow you out.'

The lamp's owner relit the lamp.

(Switch the lamp back on.)

Then he said to the lamp, 'How dare you compare your brightness to that of the stars and the moon? Their light shines for ever. They have been shining since before you were made and will still shine long after you have been broken. They shine through all kinds of weather. Your light can be blown out by the merest of breezes.'

The fighting cocks and the eagle

Two cockerels were fighting in the farmyard.

After a hard struggle, the loser went into the corner of the hen house to lick his wounds.

The winner went up onto a high wall and started to flap his wings and crow. An eagle soaring by was attracted by the noise and pounced on the winner carrying him off.

The defeated bird came out. From then on he was ruler of the farmyard.

Ask the pupils what they think the moral behind these fables might be. *Pride comes before a fall.*

You could relate this to the proverb in the Bible: 'Pride leads to destruction, and arrogance to downfall.'

[*Proverbs 16:18*]

Conclusion

Talk to the pupils about occasions in life when pride in what they have done can be a good thing, but also about times when stubborn pride can lead them into problems.

Follow-up activity

- Ask the pupils to produce an illustrated poster of the saying 'Pride comes before a fall.'

A man and his five sons

Theme
More can be achieved by working together than by working alone

Materials
- A single sheet of paper
- A local telephone directory

Assembly organization
Ask for two volunteers. Give one the single sheet of paper and the other the telephone directory. Ask each of the volunteers to tear up the paper they have been given.

Ask the pupils why one volunteer can tear up the single piece of paper but the other cannot tear up the telephone directory. *A single sheet of paper is not very strong but many sheets of paper together are very strong.*

Tell the pupils the following fable to illustrate the point. If you wish, a group of pupils could act out the story as you tell it. Explain that at the end you would like someone to tell you the moral.

A man and his five sons
A man once had five sons who were always arguing and fighting. One day the man became so fed up with his sons' behaviour that he decided to teach them a lesson. He went out and collected five twigs of the same size and tied them all together. When he had done this, he called his sons together and said, 'Can any of you take this bundle of sticks and break it?'

The man's eldest son replied, 'I can do that easily.'

The father gave his son the bundle and he tried to break it. Try as hard as he might, the son could not break the twigs. After a while the eldest son handed the bundle back to his father and said, 'It's impossible.'

One after another each of the sons tried to break the bundle of twigs, but they all failed.

After the last of his sons had failed to break the bundle the father said, 'Now let me show you how it is done.'

He undid the bundle and gave one twig to each of his sons. He told them to break the twig, which of course they could do. The father went on to explain that they are like the twigs. On their own they can be broken, but if they all work together they are too strong.

Ask the pupils what they think is the moral of this story. *We can achieve more when we work together than we can on our own.*

Conclusion

Talk to the pupils about occasions when it is important that they work together as a team, as it enables them to achieve as much as possible.

Follow-up activity

- Start by holding a brief discussion on the important aspects of working in a team, for example:

- listening to other people's ideas

- agreeing on a solution to the problem

- sharing the work fairly.

- Ask the pupils to work in teams. Give each team ten sheets of newspaper and 60 cm of Sellotape.

- Working in their teams, the pupils have to build the tallest free-standing structure they can, using only the materials they have been given.

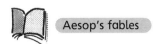

The stag and the pool

Theme

What is of most worth is not always of most value

Materials

- OHP and screen
- OHT 2 'The stag'
- Two envelopes: one labelled '£1,000,000', with a piece of paper explaining that the person is very rich, but in very poor health, paralysed from the neck down, and only able to move in a special wheelchair; the other labelled 'Health', with a piece of paper explaining that the person lives in a small house, but is very healthy and plays a number of different sports at least once a week.

Assembly organization

Ask for two volunteers to come out to the front. Let one choose one of the two envelopes. Give the other envelope to the second volunteer. Ask them if they are happy with their envelopes.

Project the OHT 2 onto a screen. Refer to the picture on the screen whilst telling the following fable of the stag.

The stag and the pool

A stag was drinking in a pool one day. When he saw his reflection he thought, 'What a fine pair of antlers I have, but it's a shame my legs are so thin.'

At this point the stag saw a lion creeping towards him. The stag turned and started to run across the open ground. He left the lion far behind.

When the stag entered the woods he was far ahead of the lion, but in the wood he could not move as fast because his antlers kept getting caught in the branches. Soon the lion caught up with him.

Ask the pupils questions to bring out the moral of the story.

Which part of his body did the stag admire? *His antlers.*
Which part of his body had been of most help to him? *His legs.*

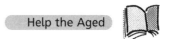

order to abandon ship. With the outside temperature at −40°C, the men spent their first night on the ice in thin linen tents.

Finally, on 21 November 1915, *Endurance* sank. Almost all the expedition's food, all their warm clothing and their radio equipment went down with the ship, but they did save three lifeboats. One crew member wrote:

'We were in a mess, and the boss was the man who could get us out.'

Shackleton told the crew that they would have to march 640 km over the ice to Paulet Island, dragging with them all their supplies and the lifeboats, each of which weighed a ton.

Dragging the boats proved to be impossible, so Shackleton decided they would make camp and wait until they could launch the boats. They survived on a diet consisting mainly of penguin and seal meat. Blubber from the seals provided their fuel.

On 9 April 1916, the ice began to break up and Shackleton gave the order to launch the boats. They sailed for Elephant Island. Day and night in temperatures of −23°C they sailed through mountainous seas, which washed over the boat, soaking the men. In these conditions their clothing froze solid. For most of the time at sea, knowing the importance of showing his men that he was in charge, Shackleton stood, at the stern of his little boat. Eventually on 15 April they landed on Elephant Island, a barren island, where 128 km per hour winds tore their tents to pieces, forcing them to sleep in the boats.

As no one knew where they were they were still not safe. So Shackleton decided to set sail once again with five others and to reach the whaling station on South Georgia, some 1280 km away. They sailed for seventeen days, during which time once again their soaked clothes froze and their drinking water turned brackish (salty and undrinkable).

When they did reach South Georgia, they were still 241 km by sea and 35 km by land, over mountains, from the whaling station. Shackleton decided to set out with two others to take the overland route and, at 3 a.m. on 19 May, with screws through the soles of their shoes to give them grip, they set off.

After 36 hours without rest, on 20 May 1916, Shackleton reached the whaling station. A ship was sent immediately to pick up the rest of the party from South Georgia and finally, on 30 August 1916, after four attempts, Shackleton reached Elephant Island and rescued the rest of his men.

Conclusion

Point out to the pupils that, although he had failed in his aim to cross the Antarctic continent, through his endurance and determination Ernest Shackleton had saved his own life and those of the other 27 men in his crew. This achievement can serve as a message to us all not to give up when faced with difficulties.

Follow-up activity

- Ask the pupils to write a diary of Shackleton's thoughts and his conversations with the crew about the ordeal that faces them, as the *Endurance* sinks. Remember to be positive and give encouragement as Shackleton might have done.

- A less challenging activity would be to produce an illustrated poster of Shackleton's family motto: By endurance we conquer.

Abraham Lincoln and William Wilberforce

Theme
Human rights

Materials
- Two large sheets of paper, each with one of the following names on one side of it and the relevant facts on the other:
  - **Abraham Lincoln**
    He was born in Kentucky in 1809
    He was elected President of the United States
    He led the North in the American Civil War, in the fight against slavery
    He was assassinated in 1865
  - **William Wilberforce**
    He was born in Kingston-upon-Hull in 1759
    He was elected Member of Parliament for Hull
    He was a pioneer member of the anti-slavery movement and founder of the Society for the Abolition of the Slave Trade
    He died in 1833

Assembly organization
Ask for two volunteers to hold up the signs. Either read the facts about the two people yourself, or let the volunteers read them from the back of their sheets.

Ask the pupils what the connection is between these two people. *They both fought against the slave trade.*

Explain to the pupils that the slave trade started in the early 1500s and ended in the mid-1800s and that during that time twelve million Africans were taken from their homes and sold into slavery in the Americas.

Talk to the pupils about the attempts by the United Nations to outlaw all such abuses of human rights.

Following the Second World War, when the Nazis used slave labour, the United Nations produced 'The Declaration of Human Rights'.

This was an attempt to try to prevent this sort of thing from ever happening again. Article 4 of this declaration states:

'No one shall be held in slavery; slavery and the slave trade shall be prohibited in all their forms.'

(This statement could be read out by a volunteer.)

Talk to the pupils about the other things they think should be basic human rights.

Privacy of your home	Freedom of movement
Freedom of thought	Freedom of speech
Freedom of religious opinion	The freedom to choose where to live
The right to an education	The right to a fair trial
The right to protection under the law	The right to equal treatment under the law
The right to work	The right to leisure time
The privacy of post	

Conclusion

Remind the pupils that we should be thankful for the work done by people like Lincoln and Wilberforce in stopping the immoral slave trade. We should also be thankful for the fact that we live in a country where our human rights (as set out originally in the United Nations Declaration of Human Rights) are respected. We should spare a thought for those people who still live in countries where their human rights are not respected. At this point you might like to draw the pupils' attention to some specific events which have made the national news, where people's rights are not being respected.

Follow-up activity

- Hold a class discussion on the rights pupils feel they should have within the school for example:
  - to be free from bullying
  - not to be caned by teachers
  - to have a warm school
  - to have clean classrooms
- Following this discussion the pupils can write up a list of rights they feel apply to the school.

Terry Waite

Theme
Having the strength to withstand personal suffering

Materials
- Two large sheets of paper, each with one of the following written on it:
  - Hostage
  - Terry Waite.

Assembly organization
Ask for two volunteers to come to the front and hold up the two signs.

Ask the pupils these questions.

- What is the connection between the two signs? *Terry Waite was taken hostage in the 1980s.*
- What does the word 'hostage' mean? *Someone who is taken and held against their will.*

Explain about the events which took place, leading up to Terry Waite being taken hostage, and then the events that happened during his time as a hostage.

Terry Waite – Hostage
In the 1980s different groups of people were being taken hostage in the area of the world called the Middle East (Iran, Libya and Lebanon).

Terry Waite went to Iran and Libya as an envoy from the Archbishop of Canterbury and successfully negotiated the release of these hostages.

Once again, when hostages were taken in the Lebanon, Terry Waite was asked to go and try to negotiate their release. Despite fears for his own safety, he went to try to help. During these negotiations Terry Waite was taken hostage himself.

At the start of his ordeal Terry Waite decided to keep three thoughts in mind:

- have no regrets
- have no false sentimentality
- have no self pity.

For the majority of his time as a hostage (nearly four years), Terry Waite was kept on his own. In the early days he had no books, radio or television and he had to think of things to keep his mind occupied. One of the things he did was to remember the words of Lord Byron's poem, *The Prisoner of Chillon*.

My hair is grey, but not with years,
My limbs are hard, though not with toil.
I suffer chains and courted death.

Explain to the pupils that, as in the poem, Terry Waite was often kept in chains and allowed no exercise.

Finally, on 18 November 1991, after a total of 1763 days (nearly four years) as a hostage, much of which he was kept in solitary confinement chained to a radiator, Terry Waite was released.

Conclusion

Talk to the pupils about the tremendous personal strength Terry Waite must have had to endure this ordeal. Remind them that we can all learn, from his example, to face our own difficulties in life with similar determination.

Follow-up activity

- Imagine Terry Waite is a hostage now. Write a letter to him, encouraging him to survive his ordeal and reassuring him that one day he will be set free.

- In your letter you might also like to tell him about certain events that have been happening in the world, which you think might help to encourage him and to cheer him up.

Simon Weston

Theme

Success despite personal suffering; forgiveness

Materials

None necessary

Assembly organization

Familiarize the pupils with a few facts about the Falklands War.

Where are the Falkland Islands? *In the South Atlantic off the coast of Argentina.*

When was the Falklands War? *1982.*

Who was Britain at war with over the Falkland Islands? *Argentina.*

The Falklands War

After the Falkland islands had been invaded by the Argentinians, the British Government sent a task force to recapture the islands, as it was the wish of the people of the Falkland Islands to remain under British rule. During the six weeks of fighting, 255 Britons and 652 Argentinians were killed and many more were seriously injured.

Talk about the injuries suffered by Simon Weston. You could talk about the events leading up to his injuries and then ask if anyone can name the individual.

Simon Weston

On 8 June 1982, Simon Weston was aboard the transport ship *Sir Galahad*, which was moving troops around the islands.

The *Sir Galahad* was hit by a 2000 pound bomb. Fifty-one service personnel were killed and many more were seriously injured, one of whom was Simon Weston. As a result of the fire on board he suffered terrible burns.

In his own words, Simon Weston describes what happened to him:

'Pain drew my eyes to the backs of my hands and I watched, transfixed by horror, as they fried and melted, the skin bubbling and flaking away from the bone.'

In fact his injuries were so bad that at one point, while he was still under the decks, Simon wanted to shoot himself, as many others had done.

Despite the pain he suffered Simon Weston survived his ordeal, but then had many months of suffering and painful operations to endure.

Ask the pupils how they would have felt and how they think Simon Weston felt. *Angry, annoyed, bitter, sad, depressed.*

It took Simon a long time to come to terms with what had happened to him. Eventually, instead of giving up, he decided to be positive about the rest of his life. He started raising money for injured service personnel and disadvantaged groups.

In 1987 he moved to Liverpool where he met a group of youngsters who had no work and who seemed to have no purpose to their lives. To help such groups, in 1988 Simon Weston founded the charitable organization Weston Spirit, which aimed to challenge groups of young people and encourage them to work with those less fortunate than themselves.

In 1991, nine years after he suffered his injuries, Simon Weston returned to the Falkland Islands. He hoped this would encourage a wave of tolerance and understanding between the two peoples who had, at one time, been enemies.

Conclusion

Talk about the two things we can all learn from Simon Weston's life:

- not giving up in the face of personal difficulty
- forgiveness of others.

You could relate this to the Biblical ideal of love for enemies.

[Luke 6:27–36]

Follow-up activity

- Remind the pupils that in 1991 Simon Weston returned to the Falkland Islands and met Argentinian men who had fought in the war against him.

- Ask the pupils to write a diary of what they think his feelings were before, during and after he met these men.

Dick Whittington (Lord Mayor of London)

Theme

Success through hard work and perseverance

Materials

- Sixteen large pieces of paper, each with one word from the following sayings written on it:
  - You • don't • get • anything • for • nothing.
  - If • at • first • you • don't • succeed • try, • try, • try • again.

Assembly organization

Ask for sixteen volunteers to come to the front and hold up, in the wrong order, the pieces of paper which make up the sayings. Ask another volunteer to come forward and rearrange the words into two separate sayings.

Explain to the pupils that these sayings relate to the life of a famous English character. Go on to tell them the story of Dick Whittington's life. As you tell the story relate the relevant parts of it to the sayings.

This is an ideal assembly for a volunteer to mime the parts of the story as you tell them.

The life of Dick Whittington

Dick Whittington lived during the fourteenth and fifteenth centuries. He was the son of a knight and lived in a village in Gloucester. As a young boy he was told stories of the streets of London being paved with gold. Dick Whittington decided to go to London and make his fortune.

When he arrived in London Dick was very disappointed as he found the streets were not made of gold, therefore it would not be easy for him to make his fortune.

(Relate this to the saying: 'You don't get anything for nothing'.)

Cold and hungry, Dick wandered the streets of London until he was found and given a job by a local merchant. His job was working in

the merchant's house, in the kitchens cleaning up. He still didn't have a happy life. The cook was very cruel to Dick and at nights he had to sleep in the attic surrounded by rats.

To help himself sleep Dick bought a cat, who turned out to be a wonderful rat-catcher and soon got rid of all the rats in the attic where Dick had to sleep.

One day Dick's merchant master asked if he would like to send anything on one of his ships, explaining that if he did he could share in the profits from the voyage. Dick decided the only thing he had was his cat so he sent that.

Dick now started to save his money to buy another cat but, fed up with the cruel treatment he received from the cook, one morning he decided to leave London.

As he left London, Dick heard the sound of the bells of Bow Church. He thought they were telling him to 'Turn again'. He turned back and returned to his job. When he returned, Dick learnt that his cat had prevented the rats from eating the food on the ship and in return he had been sent a fortune.

(Relate this to the saying: 'If at first you don't succeed try, try, try again.')

Dick had indeed made his fortune. He married the merchant's daughter and then went on to become Lord Mayor of London three times.

Conclusion

Remind the pupils that Dick Whittington didn't, as he had hoped, get something for nothing. He only made his fortune by not giving up. Finally, relate these two points to the pupils' progress and achievements in school.

Follow-up activity

- Remind the pupils of the two sayings related to this assembly, then hold a short class discussion about how and when these sayings are relevant to their lives.

- Ask the pupils to produce an illustrated poster of one of the sayings.

Emmeline Pankhurst

Theme

Democratic rights for all people

Materials

- A large sheet of paper with the name 'Emmeline Pankhurst' written on it
- Two large sheets of paper, each with one of the following written on the front and the word 'false' written on the back:
  - First TV cook
  - Owner of Mothercare
- One large sheet of paper with the following written on the front and the word 'true' written on the back:
  - Equal rights activist

Assembly organization

Ask one volunteer to come to the front and hold up the sign saying 'Emmeline Pankhurst'. Ask three more volunteers to come out to hold up the other three signs. Ask the pupils to decide which of the three things they think is the reason for Emmeline Pankhurst's fame. Keep the correct answer until last.

Go back over the three possible answers. For each one, ask the pupils to show, by putting their hands up, if they think it is the correct answer. Turn the sign round to show the answer 'true' or 'false'.

Having established that Emmeline Pankhurst was an equal rights activist, tell the pupils about the work she and others did to gain the right to vote for women.

Emmeline Pankhurst

At the turn of the nineteenth century women did not have the right to vote. Votes for women were even opposed by Queen Victoria. Emmeline Pankhurst and others fought for women to have the same voting rights as men.

In 1889 Emmeline Pankhurst helped to found the Women's Franchise League which, five years later, helped gain women the right to vote in local elections.

In 1903 Emmeline Pankhurst and her daughter founded the Women's Social and Political Union. Their aim was to fight more vigorously for the rights of women to vote (called 'suffrage'), and their motto was 'Deeds not words'.

In 1906 the British newspapers used the word 'suffragettes' as an insult, but the suffragettes themselves were delighted by the term.

Emmeline Pankhurst organized protest marches and meetings. In 1908 she organized a demonstration at the House of Commons, at which she was arrested for refusing to keep the peace.

While in prison Emmeline Pankhurst and other suffragettes went on hunger strike. They were force fed, which was a painful process that could cause serious injury.

To gain attention for their cause the suffragettes actions became more and more violent. They:

- chained themselves to railings near 10 Downing Street
- tried to set fire to buildings and letter boxes
- fought with police outside Buckingham Palace.

In1913, Emily Dawson even threw herself at the feet of the King's horse during the Epsom Derby.

When the First World War broke out in 1914, the women took up the jobs men had been doing. After the war, in recognition for their work, women over thirty were given the vote. Finally, in May 1928, a month after Emmeline Pankhurst had died, women were given equal voting rights with men.

Conclusion

Talk to the pupils about the important role played by Emmeline Pankhurst in gaining equal voting rights for women. Remind them to be thankful that we live in a free democratic country, where we can vote for whom we wish and are free to express our opinions.

Follow-up activity

- Divide the class into small groups and ask them to discuss and decide on the correct answers to the work on the sheet 'Britain – Democracy or Monarchy'.

- After the discussion bring the class together and discuss the correct answers, giving examples of countries which have adopted each system.

Britain – Democracy or Monarchy

Match the correct meaning to the different types of state. Write your answers in the spaces below.

A state ruled by one person in total control	A system of government which represents the whole population
A state in which all property is owned by the people	A state ruled by king or queen

Democracy _____

_____

Communism _____

_____

Monarchy _____

_____

Dictatorship _____

_____

Now answer these two questions.

What is the role of the monarch in Britain?

       Ruler   Figure head   Nothing at all

Choose the correct answer from the three alternatives.

Which system of government does Britain have? _____

Prince Llewellyn

Theme

Anger – the problems it can cause

Materials

None necessary

Assembly organization

Read the following proverb from the Bible to the pupils, or ask a pupil to read it.

'People with hot tempers do foolish things; wiser people remain calm.'

[*Proverbs 14:17*]

Talk to the pupils about an example of a person who lost his temper and did a foolish thing.

Prince Llewellyn

Prince Llewellyn lived over 600 years ago, at a time when the countryside was covered in forests full of wild animals. He loved to go hunting with his dogs. His favourite was called Gelert.

One day Prince Llewellyn decided to go hunting, but as there were fierce wolves about he left Gelert behind to protect his young son, who was asleep in his bed.

When Prince Llewellyn returned from his hunting trip Gelert, covered in blood, came out to meet him. Horrified, Prince Llewellyn rushed into his castle looking for his son. All he saw was his son's bed in a mess and blood everywhere.

Ask the pupils what they think Prince Llewellyn thought had happened. *Gelert had gone wild, attacked and killed his son.* What do they think Prince Llewellyn did next? *Killed Gelert.* Continue to tell the story.

In a fit of anger Prince Llewellyn took his sword and plunged it into Gelert's heart, killing the animal instantly.

Ask the pupils if they can think of anything else that might have happened? *Gelert had been protecting the young son and had had a fight with a wolf which had come into his bedroom.* Return to the original story.

As Prince Llewellyn plunged his sword into Gelert's heart he heard the cries of his son from under the bed covers.

When he went over to investigate the cries he found his son underneath the bedding. On the other side of the bed he saw the dead body of a wolf. Only at this point did Prince Llewellyn realize the truth of what had happened but it was too late, Gelert was already dead.

Conclusion

Remind the pupils that, to avoid making a mistake as in the story of Prince Llewellyn, they should always avoid reacting in anger. You could also talk to the pupils about some of the situations where they could become angry, and the best ways to deal with them.

Follow-up activity

- Write a brief story, it can be about a real or imaginary incident, in which you lose your temper and things go wrong.

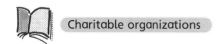

Charitable organizations

The work of charitable organizations provides ideal material to encourage the pupils to think of others less fortunate than themselves, or to think of the environment, hence helping in their moral development. Charitable organizations can also be used to reinforce the pupils' cultural development, as some of them have been part of the British Cultural Heritage for a number of years. It is even possible to give these assemblies a spiritual element by using one of the following Biblical passages on charity.

Matthew 6:1–4   Teaching about charity
Luke 21:1–4   The widow's offering

In addition, these assemblies can be given extra meaning by using them at a time when a national or international event has occurred in which the charity of your choice is involved. You could also use one of these assemblies as part of a school-based charity event to raise money for that charity.

Assembly	Theme
Help the Aged	Consideration for the elderly
Barnardo's Charity	Helping less fortunate children
The Royal National Institute for the Blind	Thinking of those less fortunate than you
Oxfam	The suffering of the poor peoples of the world
The International Red Cross	Caring for people in a crisis
The Royal National Lifeboat Institution	The work of the RNLI
The Royal Society for the Protection of Birds	Protection of British bird species and their environment
Save the Children	Thinking of those less fortunate than ourselves
World Wide Fund For Nature	Worldwide plant and animal conservation
Friends of the Earth	Environmental protection
Shelter	Homelessness

Help the Aged

Theme
Consideration for the elderly

Materials
- OHP and screen
- OHT 4 'Help the Aged logo'

Assembly organization
Display the OHT on the screen, but cover up the name of the organization, so that the pupils can only see the logo. Ask the pupils if anyone can name this charity.

Tell the pupils a little about how Help the Aged was founded.

Help the Aged
The organization was set up in 1961 to help older people suffering from disasters around the world. In 1964 the charity widened its activities to include helping older people in Britain.

Help the Aged's aim was, and still is:
'To improve the lives of elderly people around the world and in Britain.'

Here are some of the problems faced by older people in Britain today.
- Over four million older people have a disability of some sort.
- One in every ten people over 60 are blind or partially-sighted.
- One in every three older people have problems with their hearing.
- Half the people aged 75 and over live alone.
- One and a half million older people are alone and lonely at weekends.

At which two special times of the year do you think the problem of loneliness might be saddest for older people? *Christmas and birthdays.*

- 1 in 20 older people spend Christmas alone.
- Many older people get no presents or cards on their birthdays.

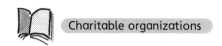

(This point can be emphasized by reading out the following quote.)

'Sometimes I go for a whole week without talking to anyone.'

What time of the year do you think could be most dangerous for older people? *Winter.*

Many older people have to choose between heating their homes or eating food, both of which are vital for life. Very cold weather in winter can cause up to 25,000 older people to die.

(This point can be emphasized by reading out the following quote.)

'All I have is a gas fire but I can't afford to put it on for very long.'

Help the Aged work to improve the lives of older people in Britain. They:

- run homes for older people
- provide specially adapted mini buses
- provide and fit home security kits.

Conclusion

Talk to the pupils about being thankful for the work being done by Help the Aged to help older people today and to be respectful and thoughtful themselves towards older people.

Follow-up activity

- Ask the pupils to write a diary for a special day (Christmas, Easter or birthday) in the life of a pensioner.

- What do they do? What do they have to eat? Who do they talk to on that day? What do they think about?

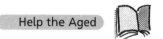

OHT 4 'Help the Aged logo'

Help the Aged

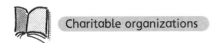

Barnardo's Charity

Theme
Helping less fortunate children

Materials
None necessary

Assembly organization
Talk to the pupils about the early life of Thomas Barnardo, leading up to his formation of the Barnardo's Charity.

Barnardo's Charity
Thomas John Barnardo was born in Dublin in 1845.

He planned to become a medical missionary in China. In 1866 he left Ireland to train as a doctor in London.

He soon realized that there was work for him to do in London, where thousands of children slept on the streets. Many of them had been injured working in the factories. As many as one in five of these children died before they were five years old.

One night Barnardo met a young orphan called Jim Jarvis who was looking for a place to sleep. Barnardo told him to go home to his mother and father. Jim took Barnardo to see where he and many others slept, on the shed roofs down backstreets.

Barnardo gave up his plans to go to China. In 1868 he set up the East End Juvenile Mission for Children. Shortly afterwards he set up a home for boys at 18 Stepney Causeway, London.

At the start the number of places in Barnardo's homes was limited. This changed after a boy nicknamed 'Carrots' was refused a place and Barnardo later found that he had died. From then on Barnardo had a sign put above all his homes which said:
'No destitute child ever refused admission.'

Barnardo's work soon changed as he started caring for girls as well as boys.

During his life Barnardo rescued 60,000 children from conditions of terrible poverty and he helped 250,000 more.

John Thomas Barnardo died in 1905, but the charity he founded carries on with the work he started.

Talk to the pupils about the work done today by Doctor Barnardo's Charity, which falls into six categories:

- Helping children with difficulties to give them a better chance.
- Helping disadvantaged children to get a good education.
- Finding foster families for children. (Barnardo's no longer run homes for children.)
- Providing help and support for people living in poor and run-down areas.
- Helping young people who are finding the change from childhood to adulthood difficult, many of whom may be homeless.
- Providing help for families with young children.

Conclusion

Talk to the pupils about being thankful for the work being done by Barnardo's Charity to help children with problems. Encourage them to think of those children who are less fortunate than they are.

Follow-up activity

- Ask the pupils to write a brief explanation of the advantages in Barnardo's trying to put children with foster families, rather than in large homes.

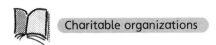

The Royal National Institute for the Blind

Theme

Thinking of those less fortunate than you

Materials

- OHP and screen
- OHT 5 'Braille'
- A table
- A chair
- A book

Assembly organization

Ask for four volunteers to come to the front. Ask two of them to carry out one of the following simple tasks:

- walk in a straight line
- sit at the table and open the book at page 20.

After these volunteers have carried out the tasks, ask them how easy they found them. Ask which sense they used to help them carry out their tasks. *Sight.*

Talk about the many things that we find easy that would become very difficult if you lost your sense of sight.

Ask the other two volunteers to carry out the same two simple tasks, but this time they should do them with their eyes closed. You could provide a blindfold, to make it more realistic.

Talk about the difficulties they have, for example, walking in a straight line, walking carefully and not bumping into anything, finding the table, the chair, the book and then the correct page.

Ask the pupils what blind people use to help them when they are walking. *A white cane.*

Ask the pupils which system of reading helps people who are blind? *Braille.*

Talk to the pupils about how The Royal National Institute for the Blind was founded and how Braille was adopted in Britain.

Doctor Armitage – founder of The Royal National Institute for the Blind

Having trained to become a doctor, Thomas Armitage was forced to leave his chosen career when he continued to have problems with his sight.

Armitage decided that he would set about finding the best system of reading and writing for blind people. He pointed out that the people best qualified to decide what would be most suited to the blind were blind people themselves.

In 1868 Thomas Armitage enlisted the help of three other blind people and formed the British and Foreign Blind Association for promoting the Education of the Blind. This became known as The Royal National Institute for the Blind.

After approximately two years they settled on the Braille system of reading and writing.

Display OHT 5 on the screen. Explain to the pupils how the Braille system works. Point out that each letter is represented by the pattern of raised dots shown on the screen.

Once Braille was adopted the Royal National Institute for the Blind started to publish material in Braille. Now they produce books, magazines, exam papers, music and even bank statements and bills in Braille.

As well as being one of the largest publishers of Braille in Europe, The Royal National Institute for the Blind supports people with loss of sight in a number of other ways:

- training for them to develop new skills
- designing products to help them (white canes, Braille watches...)
- running residential homes for elderly blind people who can no longer live on their own
- producing talking books (books recorded onto tapes for blind people to listen to): this started in 1935 and today has 90,000 members with 10,000 recorded books.

As well as these services, The Royal National Institute for the Blind helps pay for research into the prevention of blindness.

Conclusion

Remind the pupils that they should be thankful for their sight. They should think of those less fortunate than themselves who have lost their sight or have only partial sight.

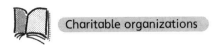

Follow-up activity

- Ask the pupils to work with a partner to ensure they are safe.

- Let one in each pair put on a blindfold and carry out a number of simple activities, such as pouring a glass of water, walking along a corridor, opening a book.

OHT 5 'Braille'

A ⠁

B ⠃

C ⠉

D ⠙

E ⠑

F ⠋

G ⠛

H ⠓

I ⠊

J ⠚

K ⠅

L ⠇

M ⠍

N ⠝

O ⠕

P ⠏

Q ⠟

R ⠗

S ⠎

T ⠞

U ⠥

V ⠧

W ⠺

X ⠭

Y ⠽

Z ⠵

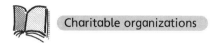

Oxfam

Theme
The suffering of the poor peoples of the world

Materials
- OHP and screen
- OHT 6 'Oxfam logo'
- Five large sheets of paper, each with one of the following words written on it:
  - Oxford • Committee • for • Famine • Relief

Assembly organization
Display the OHT on the screen, to show the pupils the Oxfam logo.

Ask for five volunteers to come out to the front and hold the sheets, without showing what is written on them. Each part of the name should be turned round and shown to the pupils when the correct answers are given.

Ask the pupils these questions.
- Which English town's name can they see in the logo? *Oxford.*
- Which other word can they see in the logo? *Famine.*

Explain to the pupils that the full name for the charity Oxfam is:

Oxford Committee for Famine Relief

At this point ask the volunteers to show the pupils all the words in the name.

Explain a little of the history behind the founding of Oxfam.

Oxfam
Oxfam was founded in 1942, when during the Second World War the Allies stopped food from reaching Greece. Civilians, including children, were starving to death.

In 1943 Oxfam raised £12,700 in relief aid for Greece.

After the war Oxfam continued to raise money to help the millions of refugees. The first Oxfam Shop was opened in Broad Street in Oxford.

Oxfam's aim was to relieve suffering caused by wars or other causes around the world.

Today Oxfam International is a worldwide charitable organization raising millions of pounds.

During the 1960s Oxfam changed the direction of the work it did, from merely emergency relief to providing long-term support, which helped people to help themselves.

- In Ethiopia, where people have suffered terrible droughts leading to starvation, Oxfam works with local organisations to provide millions of trees, which can be planted alongside the crops. These will help to hold the soil in place and provide shade.
- In the Sudan, where people risk disease from having to drink from unclean water supplies, Oxfam helps the local people dig fresh water wells.

Ask the pupils why they think it is better to provide long-term support rather than just emergency relief. *It supports the people who want to help themselves and make life better for themselves and their families. It can help to solve the problem and so prevent it from coming back.*

Conclusion

Talk to the pupils about being thankful for the work being done by Oxfam and to be thankful that they are not one of the:

- one in four people around the world who live in terrible poverty
- 800 million people who go to sleep hungry and so are at risk from disease.

Follow-up activity

- Hold a brief class discussion about the main points covered in the assembly.
- What does the name Oxfam stand for?
- What does Oxfam try to do?
- Ask the pupils to design a new logo for the Oxfam charity.

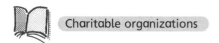

OHT 6 'Oxfam logo'

The International Red Cross

....

Theme

Caring for people in a crisis

Materials

- Seven large sheets of paper, each with one of the following words written on it:
- Humanity   • Impartiality   • Neutrality   • Independence
- Voluntary   • Unity   • Universality
- Another large sheet of paper on which has been drawn a large red cross

Assembly organization

Ask for a volunteer to come to the front of the assembly and hold up the red cross.

Ask the pupils which organization this symbol represents. *The Red Cross.*

Explain to the pupils how the Red Cross was founded.

Henri Dunant – founder of the Red Cross

When Henri Dunant (a Swiss businessman) saw the suffering of 40,000 men, from both sides, who were left to die following the Battle of Solferino in 1859, he suggested founding a national relief society.

Dunant's idea was to train volunteers to provide neutral and impartial help to relieve suffering during war. In 1863 a committee was established in Geneva. Its symbol was a red cross on a white background. (In some countries, a red crescent is used instead of a red cross.)

In 1864 the Swiss Government called a convention on the conduct of war, and the Red Cross helped in the writing of what was to become the Geneva Convention, within which the Red Cross has a unique role to offer humanitarian support to victims on both sides.

Explain that the Red Cross was founded on seven principles.

As you mention each of the principles ask a volunteer to come forward and hold up the appropriate sign. Each of these principles could be read out by volunteers.

1 Humanity
   The Red Cross exists to help and protect people who are suffering.

2 Impartiality
   The Red Cross helps those in need, whoever they are.

3 Neutrality
   The Red Cross does not take sides.

4 Independence
   The Red Cross does what it thinks best and does not take note of what others say.

5 Voluntary
   The Red Cross does its work out of commitment to others, not for money.

6 Unity
   The Red Cross welcomes everyone who wants to join and tries to help anyone in need.

7 Universality
   The Red Cross works together throughout the world, to help those in need.

Talk about the examples of the work done today by the Red Cross, you could use a large world map to show the pupils where each country is.

Montserrat

Following the volcanic eruption in 1996 the Red Cross has helped the people of the island by assisting in the building of homes and providing food.

Former Yugoslavia

After the end of the fighting during the 1990s, the Red Cross has been trying to find homes and provide food and medical supplies for the thousands of refugees.

North Korea

After the floods in 1995 the Red Cross has been providing food and medical supplies for approximately 2.6 million people.

Afghanistan

Following Afghanistan's civil war during the 1980s and 1990s the Red Crescent provided tents, water and food for refugees as well as artificial limbs for the injured.

Nigeria

The Red Cross has visited Nigerian soldiers captured by the Cameroon and taken messages back to their families.

Conclusion

Remind the pupils of the important role played by the Red Cross in helping the victims of both sides during war, and of the importance of the help they provide to people in crisis around the world.

Follow-up activity

- Ask the pupils to produce an illustrated poster to show the Red Cross's seven principles.

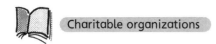

The Royal National Lifeboat Institution

Theme

The work of the RNLI

Materials

- Five large sheets of paper, each with one of the following names written on it:
- Coastguard • Police • Ambulance • Fire brigade • RNLI

Assembly organization

Ask for five volunteers to come to the front to hold up the prepared signs.

Ask the pupils these questions.

If you got into trouble in the sea, which of these services would be most likely to come and rescue you? *RNLI.*

What do the initials RNLI stand for? *Royal National Lifeboat Institution.*

Tell the pupils about the history of the RNLI.

The Royal National Lifeboat Institution

The RNLI was founded by Sir William Hillary. He lived on the Isle of Man in the nineteenth century and helped crew a boat which went out to help ships in trouble.

He was worried by the number of people who died in shipwrecks, so he wrote letters to important people, including the king, in which he suggested that every seaside town should have a boat crewed by volunteers. This became known as the Appeal to the Nation.

Sir William Hillary's appeal led to a meeting in London. As a result of this meeting, in 1824 the National Institution for the Preservation of Life was founded. In 1854 this became the Royal National Lifeboat Institution.

Since it was founded in 1824 the RNLI has saved 132,000 people.

Today the RNLI is still crewed by volunteers who are prepared to go out in all weathers to try to rescue people in danger. They are called out around 7000 times a year.

In 1998, 1500 children and teenagers got into difficulty in the sea and 400 were rescued by RNLI lifeboat crews.

To avoid becoming one of these statistics the RNLI has a four-point water safety code.

- Spot the dangers.
- Don't go alone.
- Take safety advice.
- Learn how to help.

Conclusion

Talk to the pupils about being thankful for the bravery of the RNLI crews. Remind them of the need to be careful when going to the seaside to try and ensure that they never get themselves in a position where they need to be rescued.

Follow-up activity

- Remind the pupils of the RNLI's four-point water safety code. Write each point on the board as it is mentioned.

- Ask the pupils to design a poster to illustrate the RNLI's four-point water safety code.

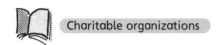

The Royal Society for the Protection of Birds

Theme

Protection of British bird species and their environment

Materials

- OHP and screen
- OHT 7 'RSPB logo'
- Eight sheets of paper, each with one of the following words written on it:
- The • Royal • Society • for • the • Protection • of • Birds
- Four more sheets of paper, each with a bird's name written on it:
- osprey • red kite • hen harrier • bittern

  (This could be enhanced if you could find pictures of the birds as well.)

Assembly organization

Display the OHT on the screen to show the pupils the RSPB logo.

Ask the pupils what the initials stand for. *The Royal Society for the Protection of Birds.*

As the answer is given, ask for eight volunteers to come to the front and hold up the society's name.

Explain a little about how The Royal Society for the Protection of Birds was founded.

The Royal Society for the Protection of Birds

The RSPB was founded in 1889 to protect birds, at which time it was known as the Society for the Protection of Birds. In 1904 it was granted a Royal Charter and became known as The Royal Society for the Protection of Birds.

Ask the pupils to identify the bird shown on the logo. *Avocet.*

The avocet was adopted as the symbol for the RSPB in 1955. It had become extinct in Britain, but coastal flooding during the Second World War resulted in the avocet returning to breed in England in 1947.

Talk to the pupils about the work of The Royal Society for the Protection of Birds today.

The work of The Royal Society for the Protection of Birds

In Britain today, some species of bird have dropped in number dramatically. This means that they could disappear from the British countryside altogether. As examples, over the last twenty years the numbers of these birds have dropped as follows:

- song thrush 73%
- skylark 54%
- tree sparrow 86%
- lapwing 50%
- grey partridge 75%

The RSPB tries to protect these and other bird species, which it does in many different ways:

- by informing people about the concerns and problems facing the birds and their environment, through magazines such as *Bird Life*

- by owning and maintaining 150 nature reserves which help to protect 30 out of 36 of Britain's threatened bird species, such as Dartford warblers, capercaillies and corncrakes

- by campaigning (talking to landowners and politicians) to protect the birds' habitats. They work with other groups to protect English lowland peat bogs. These are an endangered and a very important English habitat, where birds such as hen harriers, merlins and pink-footed geese live.

The RSPB is also working to protect remaining areas of Scottish pinewoods where the Scottish crossbill lives. This bird is found nowhere else in the world, so if this habitat disappears the Scottish crossbill will become extinct.

Talk about some specific birds and the work done by the RSPB to protect them. As you talk about each bird, ask a volunteer to come forward and hold up the bird's prepared sign.

Osprey
The osprey became extinct in Britain during the early part of this century, but then naturally re-established itself in Scotland, where there are now 125 pairs, including those at the RSPB nesting site near Loch Garten.

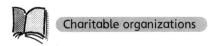

Red kite

At the beginning of this century the red kite numbers in Britain had fallen to only three or four pairs in the mid-Welsh valleys. After 1903, when the birds became a protected species, the numbers started to increase. Since 1989 the RSPB has been reintroducing red kites into other areas of Britain.

Hen harrier

In 1997 RSPB volunteers helped provide 24-hour nest-watches to protect a pair of hen harriers, which nested in Derbyshire. This is the first time hen harriers had nested there since 1870.

Bittern

Only small numbers of bitterns can be found in Britain. They live in reed beds (including the RSPB nature reserves at Minsmere and Leighton Moss). Each bittern needs an area of reed beds of 20 hectares (15 football pitches). This means that they are in danger of becoming extinct in Britain. The RSPB is trying to establish new reed beds, which will encourage the bitterns to breed elsewhere and so increase their numbers.

Conclusion

Talk to the pupils about the importance of the work done by the RSPB in protecting native British bird species and their habitats. Suggest how they could help in this work by, for example, feeding birds through the winter and not using slug pellets in gardens.

Follow-up activity

- Divide the class into small groups. Ask the pupils to think of events that are happening in Britain which are putting birds' lives in danger. After a short time bring the class together to discuss and summarize their ideas.

- Ask the pupils to produce a written summary of the things that are happening in Britain which are putting birds' lives in danger.

OHT 7 'RSPB logo'

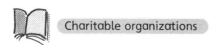

Save the Children

Theme

Thinking of those less fortunate than ourselves

Materials

- Fifteen large sheets of paper, each with one letter from the name 'Save the Children' on it

Assembly organization

Ask for fifteen volunteers to come out to the front and each hold up one of the letters. Do not show the letters to the rest of the pupils.

Ask the rest of the pupils to find the name of the charity by guessing the letters. Each time a correct letter is guessed, turn it round to show the pupils.

Once the name has been guessed, tell the pupils a little about how Save the Children was formed.

Save the Children

After the First World War, the suffering of the starving Austrian children drove Eglantyne Jebb to launch Save the Children in 1919. She believed that to get rid of the suffering caused by poverty and war, children's needs had to be met not just at a moment of crisis, but by giving them the power to help themselves.

In 1924 the League of Nations adopted the Declaration of Children's Rights, written by Eglantyne Jebb. In 1990 these rights formed part of the United Nations Convention on the Rights of the Child.

Save the Children's aims were (as they still are today):

- to fight poverty and discrimination
- to protect children from suffering caused by war and famine
- to defend the rights of children everywhere

Talk to the pupils about the work done by Save the Children today. Read out the problems and actions listed below. These could be read out by pupils.

Problems and actions

Problem	Action
Young people feel ignored and take little part in the life of their community	Save the Children helps young people get their ideas across to the people making decisions
Poor diet stunts the growth of over 400 million children	Save the Children works to prevent food shortages and help families get good food
120 million children work full-time, missing out on education	Save the Children supports schemes which reduce the need for children to work
Millions of children are killed, seriously injured or made homeless by war	Save the Children runs schemes to help children recover from the effects of war
In 1999 300,000 children were fighting in wars, some of them are as young as 10 years old	Save the Children is working to stop children under 18 fighting in wars

You could emphasize the plight of some children by reading out the story of Teku Nahn.

The life of Teku Nahn

Teku Nahn, a fourteen-year-old Liberian boy, saw soldiers come into his village, lock the door to his house and set fire to it with his brother and sister inside. Teku ran away into the bush where he survived for three months, eating wild plants. Eventually he was found by the rebel soldiers and made to join them, and to kill people. Of this experience he says:

'I killed people and sometimes today when I see orphans I feel bad, thinking maybe I killed their parents.'

Conclusion

Remind the pupils to be thankful for the work of Save the Children, helping children around the world, and to be thankful that they don't suffer the way millions of children around the world do.

Follow-up activity

- Ask the pupils to write a sentence describing the feelings of a ten-year-old child about to go into a battle for the first time.

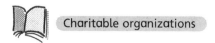

World Wide Fund For Nature

Theme
Worldwide plant and animal conservation

Materials
Three large sheets of paper, each with one of the following initials written on it:
- W   • W   • F

Assembly organization
Bring out three volunteers to hold up, in random order, the three letters.

Next ask someone to come forward and rearrange these letters to make the initials of a famous charity.

Then ask the pupils which charity these are the initials for. *World Wide Fund For Nature.*

Go on to explain to the pupils a little about the history behind the formation of the World Wide Fund For Nature.

World Wide Fund For Nature
In the 1960s people were becoming concerned about the risk of plants and animals around the world becoming extinct. Sir Julian Huxley, a scientist and conservation advisor to The United Nations, wrote:

'Many parts of Africa, which fifty years ago were swarming with game, are now bare of wildlife.'

Huxley's comment worried many people, one of whom was Victor Stolan, who wrote to him, suggesting that money should be raised, to be used to protect endangered species.

By 1961 the World Wildlife Fund (as it was known at that time) was ready to be launched. Sir Peter Scott had designed the panda logo. On 9 October 1961 the World Wildlife Fund hit the national press with the headline:

Doomed – to disappear from the face of the Earth due to man's folly, greed, neglect.

The newspaper article listed some of the thousands of plants and animals facing extinction.

Ask the pupils to name some of the animals they think might have been included in that list? *Tiger, rhinoceros, panda, blue whale, elephant…*

Although there are many animal species facing extinction, there are even more plants facing extinction:

- 6500 animals are facing extinction
- 30,000 plant species are facing extinction.

In 1986 the World Wildlife Fund changed its name to WWF – The World Wide Fund for Nature.

What do you think people were doing to put plants and animals in danger of extinction? *Killing them for food, killing them for their skins or ivory, destroying their habitat (for fire wood, to grow food), polluting their habitat.*

What do you think the WWF is doing to protect these plants and animal species? *Protecting the places where the plants and animals are found, their habitat.*

Today the WWF needs to help the peoples of the world improve their lives so that they can benefit from the protection of animals and plants. This point can be emphasized by using the following quote:.

'More than 35 years of experience has taught us that threatened species will only be saved if their habitats are protected. And habitats will only be protected if the development needs of people who share them are taken into account.'

There are many examples of the ways in which the WWF helps people improve their lives, as well as protecting plant and animal species.

- People in Africa are being helped to work with tourists to make money instead of poaching ivory.
- Instead of cutting down forests, local people are being helped to use the forests resources in a sustainable way.

In this way the plants and animals around the world can be protected, but the lives of the local people can also be improved.

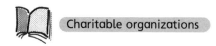

Conclusion

Talk to the pupils about the importance of conserving the plants and animals around the world. You could raise these points.

- We do not have the right to destroy these plant and animal species.
- We do not know what effect the loss of one species will have on the other plants and animals.
- We do not know if, at the same time, we are destroying any other useful plants (many drugs and foods come from plants). Some people believe that up to 1400 plant species in the rainforests could offer cures or protection against cancer.

Follow-up activity

- Divide the class up into small groups. Ask the pupils to think of the names of plants and animals that are in danger of becoming extinct and where in the world they come from.

- Bring the class together and hold a discussion to produce a list of endangered species.

- Give the pupils a world map on which they can mark the names of the species and the locations they are found.

Friends of the Earth

Theme
Environmental protection

Materials
None necessary

Assembly organization
Start by exploring the pupils' knowledge of current environmental issues and their causes. Possible areas to talk about and information to bring out include:

Environmental problem	Possible cause and effects
Global warming	Increased levels of carbon dioxide in the atmosphere could cause changes in the Earth's weather patterns.
Acid rain	Increased levels of sulphur dioxide, nitrogen oxide and other gases are causing rainwater to become more acidic; this is killing trees and fish in rivers.
Loss of ozone layer	The use of chemicals called CFCs (chlorofluorocarbons) in aerosols and fridges has been destroying the Earth's protective ozone layer; this may lead to an increase in the number of cases of skin cancer.
Over-consumption of resources	Many of the Earth's resources are being used up without thought of how they can be replaced; not enough materials such as paper, glass and metal are being recycled.
Habitat destruction	Many of the world's habitats such as rainforests and peat bogs are being destroyed; this is partly responsible for animals becoming extinct.

Environmental problem	Possible causes and effects
Pollution (air)	The over-use of cars is helping to cause air pollution, which could, some people believe, be causing increases in the incidence of asthma.
Pollution (water)	The increased use of chemical sprays could be leading to an increased level of pesticides in drinking water, lead from old water pipes could be causing health problems.

Explain to the pupils that in the 1960s and 1970s, although scientists were becoming aware of some of these problems, little was known by many members of the general public.

Ask the pupils to name some of the environmental action groups responsible for increasing public awareness of these and other environmental issues. *Friends of the Earth, Greenpeace.*

Explain to the pupils that Friends of the Earth was set up in 1971 to help protect the Earth's environment. Within a year of being set up it had over 2000 members and had set up 50 local campaigning groups.

Friends of the Earth

Friends of the Earth's first major campaign was to get the drinks manufacturer Schweppes, and others, to stop using non-returnable bottles. To publicize their belief that companies should re-use and recycle bottles, they organized the dumping of thousands of Schweppes' non-returnable bottles on the doorstep of the company's headquarters.

Today Friends of the Earth works in three ways to bring about change:

- campaigning – putting pressure on government and business to adopt environmentally sensitive policies
- citizen action – encouraging people to reduce their impact on the environment and to push governments and industries to adopt environmentally sensitive policies
- information and ideas – carrying out research and providing solutions to environmental problems, as well as circulating information.

Today Friends of the Earth campaigns to:

- protect the world's last few remaining forests and wild places
- stop pollution of the air we breathe, the water we drink and the food we eat
- protect the health of life on Earth.

Conclusion

Remind the pupils of the need to be thankful for the work of groups like Friends of the Earth. They keep us informed about problems facing the Earth and are working towards a better environment for all the planet's living things. Stress the importance of each one of us doing everything we can to reduce our own harmful effects on the planet.

Follow-up activity

- Hold a brief class discussion on the environmental problems caused by cars and lorries.

- Ask the pupils to work through the town-planning exercise and list some ways of reducing these problems.

Town-planning exercise

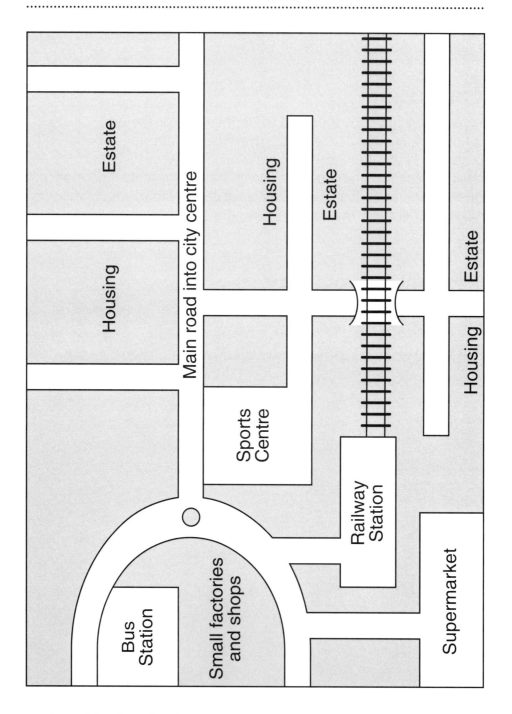

Look at this plan of a city centre.

List as many ways as you can of reducing the effects of traffic on the people.

Shelter

Theme
Homelessness

Materials
- A cardboard box

Assembly organization
Hold up the cardboard box. Ask the pupils what it can be used for. Ensure that amongst the answers that are given is: *It is used by some people to make shelters for themselves.*

Ask the pupils these questions.
- What are some of the problems faced by people living inside a cardboard box? *It is cold, it is wet, it is uncomfortable, it is not safe.*
- What other problem do homeless people face? *Hunger…*
- Which organization helps homeless people with the problems they face? *Shelter.*

Explain a little about the work done by Shelter.

Shelter
Shelter was founded in St Martin's-in-the-Fields Church on 1 December 1966, when five church housing trusts came together to publicize the plight of the homeless and to campaign for money to help relieve their suffering.

Shelter believes:

'a home is somewhere affordable, of adequate size and design, in good repair, safe and with support when needed and that to have a home is a basic human right.'

In 1999 around 900,000 families and single people were regarded as being homeless.

Emphasize to the pupils that homelessness is not just a problem of single people living in cardboard shelters. To do this you, or pupil volunteers, could read out the family stories, below.

Molly's story
Aged 87 and with her hearing deteriorating, Molly moved to live near her son. Her new house was bought in her son's name.

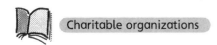

Shortly after she moved in, Molly had to go into hospital. When she got out she found her son had borrowed money, using the house as a guarantee and then not repaid any of the money he had borrowed. Now the house was going to be repossessed.

Carrie's story

Carrie, aged ten and suffering from kidney problems, lived with her mother, father and baby sister in a small one-room flat which contained her parents' bed, her sister's cot, her bed, and the kitchen. With four people living in the small room it became damp and Carrie developed asthma.

Paul's story

Paul, his parents and sister all lived in a small one-room flat. His parents both suffered from serious illnesses and depended upon Paul. At that time he was doing his A levels and found the additional stress exhausting. His parents depended upon him for everything – washing, cooking and even getting up the stairs.

Conclusion

Remind the pupils that homelessness is not something that affects only single people living rough on the streets, but that it also affects many families living in poor housing conditions. We should be grateful for the work done by Shelter to help such people.

You can reinforce this point using the following quote:

'Thanks to Shelter, I've got a little flat of my own now. I couldn't have done it without your help.'

Finally, explain to the pupils that we should be thankful for homes we have and think of those less fortunate than ourselves.

Follow-up activity

- Ask the pupils to design a poster to either:
  - encourage homeless (including those in poor houses) people to contact Shelter for help and advice

  or

  - encourage people to think of the homeless and make donations to help Shelter in their work.